THE DREAM OF THE WHALE

THE DREAM OF THE WHALE

Selected Works From the COMPAS
Writers & Artists in the Schools Program

Edited by
Florence Chard Dacey

Illustrations by
Ed Archie Noisecat

Florence Chard Dacey

COMPAS
Writers & Artists in the Schools
1994

Publication of this book is generously supported by the Lillian Wright and C. Emil Berglund Foundation, dedicated in memory of C. Emil Berglund.

COMPAS programs are made possible in part by grants provided by the Minnesota State Arts Board, through an appropriation by the Minnesota State Legislature. In the past year, the COMPAS Writers & Artists in the Schools program has received generous support from the Hugh J. Andersen Foundation, the Ashland Oil Foundation, the Lillian W. & C. Emil Berglund Foundation, U S WEST Foundation, and the First Bank System Foundation.

As always, we are grateful for the hundreds of excellent teachers throughout Minnesota who sponsor COMPAS Writers & Artists in the Schools residencies. Without their support and hard work, the writers and artists would not weave their magic, and the student work we celebrate in this book would not spring to life.

For their work in producing this book, special thanks are due to Tia Scammahorn, WAITS Program Associate; to Carol Bergeland, COMPAS Support Staff; and to Daniel Gabriel, WAITS Program Director.

ISBN 0–927663-24-4

Illustrations copyright © 1994 Ed Archie Noisecat
Music, Additional Words, Arrangements copyright © 1994 Charlie Maguire and Mello-Jamin Music
Text copyright © 1994 COMPAS
All rights reserved. No portion of this book may be reprinted or reproduced without the prior written permission of COMPAS, except for brief passages cited in reviews.

COMPAS
304 Landmark Center
75 West Fifth Street
St. Paul, Minnesota 55102

Jeff Prauer, Executive Director
Daniel Gabriel, Director, Writers & Artists in the Schools

Table of Contents

III. Give Back Hope to the Ocean

IV. Can You Still Hear the Leaves Fall?

V. TELL ME A STORY, TAKE ME AWAY

VI. TWO KINDS OF WISDOM

VII. The Sweet Clarity of Something Wonderful

INTRODUCTION

When I want to remind students of some of the elemental power of language, I ask them to try to recall the first time they urgently voiced that combination of sounds that comes out as "Mama" and the miracle occurred. She appeared. Very early, we learn words make things happen, connect us to the world. Which may be why, since early childhood, each of us has been using them to search out, devise and make connections. Perhaps you, the reader, hold this book because you too are seeking a coming together, the special kind possible through the poems, plays, songs and stories arising from the authentic beings of children.

In fact, this anthology exists because of layers of connections: A vast web of citizens in many capacities, including students' parents, relatives and friends, who support creative writing activities in their schools, homes and communities; a network of COMPAS staff, writers and artists who teach; dedicated school staff and classroom teachers; a grand company of students, from kindergarten through twelfth grade, in schools across Minnesota.

From this rich stratum come the talented student authors here, who, representing thousands more served in COMPAS residencies, have involved themselves in a complex subtle series of conjunctions. Of sense with emotion, past with present, inner with outer worlds. Using all of the tools in the writer's box, they edify and delight with their surprising combinations: a grandfather who dances in the sky, a wolf who pairs up with a cat to solve a village's problem. Such agile artistic leaping encourages us readers to collide with a new idea, revisit parts of ourselves, or reconsider the world we share.

As editor, it is my privilege to highlight yet another layer of intermingling. In choosing one piece of writing from those submitted for each week of a COMPAS writing residency, I wanted to include a variety of subjects, forms and voices. Patterns within evolving sections and the collection as a whole also influenced my selections. This process was made even more demanding by the abundance of fine writing.

The seven sections of this book tell a familiar, yet always fresh, endlessly necessary story. Each of us has been "one kid on the earth," as Jenny Quaale (Franklin Magnet School) puts it in her poem "Date on a Calendar." We are aware of our separate uniqueness and the family that brought us forth. Remember the childhood wonders, the intense moments that could make a day seem as full as a lifetime? And who hasn't felt the loss and betrayal that provoke the plea in a poem by Dan Kreuser (Pine Hill Elementary)? "Give me back my heart, so I can love again." Nature, our imagination, human wisdom and faith are some of the sources of renewal students write of so convincingly. Circling round, redefined and strengthened, we can again "face the world," as Laura Utphall (Columbia Heights Central Middle School) writes in her poem "Scribbles." Because of these valuable, valued writings, I am persuaded that any of us would profit from following the path this book illuminates. Through the words, we remember our origins and what sustains us. We name and express our pain and joy, fashion our personal and imaginary stories. We question, contemplate, reinvent our lives. We determine never to stop doing it, again and again.

I hope these writings will conjure up for you, as they do for me, a child, a group of children, nurtured enough, stalwart enough to undertake the conjoining and gathering, the knotting and splicing, bonding and bridging that end in words on a page. These are words meant to be shared, acted out, sung, told abroad in the world. Invitations to join in the grieving, the laughter, the confusion, the gratefulness, and the profound satisfactions of creative expression.

In her spirited poem on singing and dancing which ends this anthology, Jillian Hegstrom (Crestview Elementary) writes: "we're having fun, we'll never finish." This is the kind of enthusiasm COMPAS artists can awaken in students. The creative dance of language, the free pursuit of who we are, what we know and can conceive in words is exhilarating and essential. Because of it, the particular whale that is waiting for you to find it in these pages was born in the mind of Sara Polley (Greenleaf Elementary), one of countless children in COMPAS programs who felt welcomed into that creative process. I think her whale is dreaming of the freedom to be its mysterious, natural limited, yet boundless self. I think this is just the sort of sustaining dream that connects all of us with these young writers who so generously impart themselves in words.

Florence Dacey
July, 1994

A Note to Teachers

Using *The Dream of the Whale* as Source Material for Writing

The COMPAS Writers & Artists in the Schools anthology celebrates the work done by the students participating in the 1993–94 program. This book also can serve as a valuable teaching tool. Students are impressed, encouraged and stimulated when they listen to the writing of their peers.

You can work with one of the seven broad themes explored in the separate sections. Or you may choose a particular form, such as poetry, and pick out poems from throughout the book that will appeal to your students. Use the poems, stories, dramatic works and songs as models for writing and to generate discussions about elements of good prose and poetry. Consider including an appropriate selection in your study of other subjects, such as a poem about an animal in your science class. Encourage students particularly interested in creative writing to read the book on their own.

You can also read to your students from this collection in preparation for a residency by a COMPAS writer, who can demonstrate additional methods for using the the anthology in teaching.

In these and other ways of your own devising, you will greatly extend the value and influence of this student work. Thanks for this and for all you do to nurture creativity in your students.

One Kid on the Earth

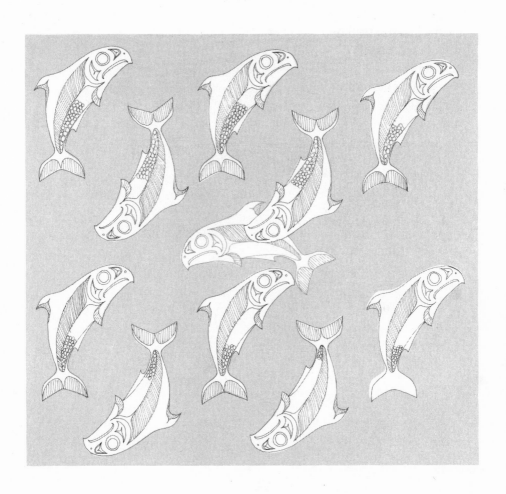

When I Was A . . .

When I was an island
my dad was the water protecting me.
When I was a heart
my mom was the love flowing through me.
When I was a basketball
my uncles were the hoop waiting to catch me before I fall.
When I was a trophy
my aunties were the hands holding me high in the air.
When I was an eagle
my grandfather helped me soar high above the clouds.
When I was an egg
my grandmother held me with tender loving care.

Paul Fox :: Grade 5
Eisenhower Elementary School :: Hopkins

It's Me

Introducing the one, the only
notoriously funny . . . Me!
He comes from a place like no other.
A place of mystery.
A place that filled him with pieces
of sports, music, jokes, knowledge.
Trained his tongue to tastes of ice cream,
pizza, candy, and occasionally a few vegetables.
Entertained him with Babe Ruth, Emmitt Smith,
Patrick Ewing.
Filled him with feelings of joy, pain, regret.
His eyes searching for the color to lighten stress.
His mouth speaking, asking, yelling, forgiving.
His ears the opening for jokes, riddles,
receiving answers of life.
No one knows where he came from.
I'd sure like to know.

Bob Hannah :: Grade 8
Oltman Junior High School :: St. Paul Park

Untitled

My name: first, last, middle.
Middle, Marie, my mother's, my grandmother's, and
    my great-grandmother's middle
    name, a strong name.
My name, a sweet child named Devie
    an irritable kid named
    Deven Marie.
Deven, my name, a poet, someone who
expresses herself.
My name, a piano, the harmony,
the style.
My name, the navy-blue night
sky.
Deven, a designer.
My name, famous cities, social events,
peaceful Australia.

Deven Nelson :: Grade 8
Rush City Schools :: Rush City

The One Who Fell into the Pond

I was the one who left
the tackle box open
and the dog got into it.

I was the one who used my sister's
roller blades without permission
and scratched them up.

I was the one who ran
over the little pine tree
with the sled.

I was the one who went into
my sister's room and went looking
in her drawers for neat things.

the one who fell into the pond
when Bobby was over.

I was the one who lost all
my sister's game pieces.

Bobby and I were the ones who
put ink on my sister's light switch
so when she touched it
she would get ink on her hand.

I was the one that would do
the dishes for a few cents.

Dustin Greenig :: Grade 5
Washington Elementary School :: Detroit Lakes

Sorry Heather

I apologize to
my sister because
when I was one
my sister had a
dog named Rusty. One
morning when my sister
was sleeping I
went downstairs
and sat on
her dog. I
shouldn't have done
it because I
almost killed the
dog. I did
it to pretend
I was a
cowgirl and the
dog was my
horse.

Jacki Johnson :: Grade 3
St. Michael-Albertville Elementary School :: St. Michael

BEST WORDS!

I'll name my favorite words
for skiing: jumps, cliffs, skis,
steep hills, extreme skiing, powder,
tree skiing. My mom's favorite
words are: You might have gotten yourself
killed.

Phil Linduska :: Grade 5
Royal Oaks Elementary School :: Woodbury

Mom

You are the stem on my rose
You are the flower in my garden
You are the apple on my tree
You are the chocolate in my candy bar
You are the peanut in my shell
You are the numbers in my math book
You are the hands on my watch.

Sarah Giese :: Grade 5
Parkway Elementary School :: St. Paul

I am healed by the sun,
wounded by my big brother,
wounded by a dog coming at me.
I am healed by my mother
making sausage.
I am wounded by my father
not paying me my money.

I am healed by my mother
taking me to the store
and buying me bubble gum.
I am healed by the smell
of roses.
I am wounded by the wind
blowing me,
cured by my big sister taking me
to the library, letting me
check out books.
I am wounded by my best friends
not playing with me.
I am healed by the Power Ranger.
I am wounded
by the monster under my bed.

Mary Yang :: Grade 3
North End Elementary :: St. Paul

THE RED AND WHITE DRAGON

When I feel mad
I turn into a red and white
fire-breathing dragon.
When I get real mad
I steam
and I make a forest fire.
I don't mean to
but I get so out of control
I can't stop.
But when my mom hears me
stomp on the floor,
she comes up and I turn
back into me.
I wonder where
my other self goes?
The dragon?

Michaela Jo Tieben :: Grade 2
Oakridge Elementary School :: Eagan

My Jurassic Park Room

I wish I could
have a big carpet
with Jurassic Park
printed on it.
I wish I could
have wallpaper with
big vicious lunging
velociraptors on it.
I wish I could
have a spitting-and-
putting-up-its-
big-frill dilophosaur
bed.
And I wish I
could have an angry gigantic
T-Rex ceiling.

Adam Thomas :: Grade 3
South Elementary School :: St. Peter

LIKE A STONE

Sometimes I am like a stone.
Hard and heavy.
But I'm really ice.

When I feel sad
I melt down and become
part of the ocean.
I'll be the wavery sound of its music
and pull you down deep.
Soon you'll discover gold
and become a sculpture that stands
for pearls and treasures.

I had two choices:
To go back on land
or stay in water with treasures.
I'm back on the sand,
and now I'm glass
that I can't hide,
an open mind
that I'll always have inside.

Julie Yang :: Grade 6
Franklin Magnet School :: St. Paul

My name is a spider weaving a shiny web in a dark corner, the wind is whistling through the web. My dream is a red bird floating through the light blue sky like a hang glider floating through the sky. My memory is the black of night when the moon comes out. My secret is the snow that falls and makes the earth as white as a cloud. My memory is a brook that fish swim in and the water shines as the sun looks down at it.

Alysa Dockry :: Grade 2
Greenleaf Elementary School :: Apple Valley

My Ideas

In my mind there is a cloud for questions.
For bad questions there is a dark cloud.
In my mind there is a typewriter that types ideas.
In my mind there is a lock, and when I get a new idea
it locks. It keeps it good and tight.

Matthew Schmitz :: Grade 1
Aquila Primary Center :: St. Louis Park

ODE TO MY HANDS

My hands grasp
around objects
not letting go
like a snake squeezing
tighter and
tighter. Like
a spider
with five legs.
Neglected,
in everyday
use, taken
advantage of.
Mysterious
noises, looks
and feelings.
Hiding it
with rings
and other
jewelry.
Grasping, holding,
squeezing . . . dry.
Lines and names.
Abused in
so many ways, yet
beautiful.

Many colors,
no noises and
never annoying, like
an animal with
manners. Beautiful
and only beautiful
by itself.

Ashley Hoene :: Grade 5
Greenleaf Elementary School :: Apple Valley

Cells are the smallest living things in your body
You find them in tissue and organs too
Organs work together to make a system
We're going to tell what the systems do
Here we go, we'll let you know
We'll tell you what the systems do

    Circulatory, pumps the blood around
    Respiratory, makes the air go down
    Digestive, takes care of your meal
    Nervous system tells you what you feel

The heart is the main part, in the middle of your chest
Pumps blood north, south, east and west
Goes to your cells to help you grow
Brings your oxygen into the flow
Here we go, to let you know
Tell you what the systems do

    (Chorus)

Open your mouth, breathe in deep
Goes down your windpipe very steep
Goes into the air sacs in your lungs
CO2 goes out past your tongue
Here we go, to let you know
Tell you what the systems do

    (Chorus)

That tasty hot dog that you chew
Gives your body a job to do
Mixes with saliva, on your tongue
Goes down your esophagus, yum, yum, yum
Here we go, to let you know
Tell you what the systems do

(Chorus)

The skin calls the brain like a telephone
It calls you up—Is there someone home?
It calls so fast, you don't even know
From the hairs on your head to the tip of your toe
Here we go, let you know
Tell you what the systems do

(Chorus)

Mrs. Johnson's Class :: Grade 4
Fillmore Central Elementary School :: Preston

Verse

Cells are the small-est liv-ing things in your bo-dy_ You

find them in tis-sue and or-gans,_ too._

Or-gans work to-ge-ther to make a sys-tem._ We're

gon-na tell you what the sys-tems_ do.

Here we_ go,_ we'll let you_ know._ We'll

tell you what the sys-tems_ do. *Chorus* Cir-cu-la-

to-ry pumps the blood a-round,_ respi-ra-

to - ry   makes the air   go   down,   di -

ges - tive _   takes   care   of your _ meal.

Ner- vous sys - tem tells   you   what   you _   feel.

INSIDE ME

Take away the smile
The body
The skin
The bones
Inside my soul
Come in, come in
I'll show you around
You'd be surprised how much
A soul can hide
Fears and pain
Anger and confusion
Keep going
Come on, don't be scared
There is so much I can hide
Pain, so much pain
What do you see?
Yes
Yes
That is it, you found it
My prized possession
My love

Nikia Colbeth :: Grade 8
Oltman Junior High School :: St. Paul Park

My Dear Sister Kimberly

My sister has a twinkle in her eye
A twinkle brighter than the stars of heaven
When I am in an empty and gloomy cave
My sister leads me out to the light by giving me a kiss
She sleeps in my arms
Her eyes shut, head on my chest
and her tiny fingers curled up
I wonder when she grows up
Will she hate me
or will she look up to me and show me her smile?
Either way, I will love her for eternity.

Viet Huynh :: Grade 5
Oakridge Elementary School :: Eagan

THE BIG SLEEP

My grandpa dances on the clouds.
He makes castles
for the Prince of Peace.
My grandpa has gone through
the gate of the big sleep.
He plays golf on the high heavens.
My grandpa helps me
across the big learning swamp.
Sometimes my grandpa talks
to the Brother of Everyone.

My grandpa sleeps
on a golden flower.
He rescues me
from Shredder when he's going to capture me.
He laughs with me
when I am playing with dinosaurs.
He takes me up
when I'm down on the bottom floor
My grandpa is as special as Kirby Puckett
when the Twins are fighting for freedom.

Vanessa Warnke :: Grade 4
Highwood Hills Elementary School :: St. Paul

I am a feather
on a bird.
I am a small
star on the flag.
I am a grain
of sand on the beach.
I am a pebble at
the bottom of
the lake.
I am a crater on
the moon.
I am one of the ashes
after the fire burns out.
I am a strand of hair
on someone's head.
I am a date on a
calendar.
I am a penny from
a dollar.
I am a snowflake in
a blizzard.
I am one kid on the earth.

Jennifer Quaale :: Grade 4
Franklin Magnet School :: St. Paul

THE PAST

Who can look through the window of the past?
When kids jumped on beds
and a little girl used daffodils as tea cups.
When little boys and girls wished on stars at night.

Marcus Moreno :: Grade 4
Ames Elementary School :: St. Paul

Dreams of the Past

In those days when dreams
were as big as rippling oceans.
Days of happiness
when I was always someone
else and never knew the world
I really lived in, celebrating
each season as it came in
little bursts of enjoyment.
Winging in to any open space
awaiting my arrival, waiting
to swallow me where I would
lose all track of time, where
idols were as much fun
making up as believing in. If only
the true roots of life would come again
as the seasons, for then we would
always be the honest children. But they
fade away as a new-fallen snow trampled
after it's been played in. Maybe
if I can be the one I was before,
from deep, from the depths of the
present me, it will all flow into me
again as the waters of pure happiness.

Chiara Schoen :: Grade 6
St. Pius X Elementary/Middle School :: White Bear Lake

In the Morning I Can Hear

In the morning I can hear my music
box playing an ice skating song. It plays
the song I ice skate that year. I can hear
baby birds chirping. I can hear my dreams falling
apart in my head and coming into my life.
I can hear a rose growing in a bush, becoming
more beautiful each day. I can hear the most beautiful
birds landing on my window sill and singing the
most beautiful songs, trying to wake me up, and when
I wake up they wait for breakfast. I can hear
the most beautiful sounds.

Iswariya (Anu) Jayachandran :: Grade 3
Homecroft Elementary School :: St. Paul

The desks wake up
and clean themselves up for the kids.
The chairs get unstacked.
Pencils get sharpened
and erasers cleaned.
All of the things stand up in the classroom
to say the pledge.
The crayons start to wrestle.
Books start to open.
And the teacher starts to appear.
The kids start to fly in.

Keli Holtmeyer :: Grade 2
Fernbrook Elementary School :: Maple Grove

Best Moment

The heat from the sun burned,
and when I stepped into the shade,
a deep cool shadow hovered over me.

I caught my breath and paced
toward the tire swing that hung
tightly onto a thick branch
connected miles up the trunk
of a huge acorn tree.

I leaped toward the swing
and spun it around several times.
It looked like a penny
that had just fallen to the floor
and was spinning frantically.

When the rope was tight
and would not spin anymore,
I jumped on.

The tire began to spin like
a massive tornado, and I was the center.
My stomach churned, I screamed.
It was a thrilling, chilling moment
I would never forget.

After what seemed forever,
the spinning turned into a slow pace.
It was peaceful sitting there
turning around slowly.
I looked above me. I saw a beautiful
mass of blended color with
greens, blues, whites and browns.

The swing was barely moving.
I stepped off and nearly fell over.
I was dizzy and my stomach was full
of butterflies. Why I enjoyed it,
I cannot say, but it was one of
my best moments in life.

Sarah Paul :: Grade 7
Oltman Junior High School :: St. Paul Park

THE FIRST ONE

The sun was fading like
a light going out. "Five minutes
left," I heard from behind. I
cast, it flew like an eagle
soaring over the trees. "Splash,"
it said as it hit the water.
In a moment I felt it
tug and I cranked. It
kept coming closer and
closer and then I saw it.
The sleek body like a race
car, its eyes were fireballs
in a mirror. It was a walleye,
the first one.

Jeff Spatafore :: Grade 5
Elm Creek Elementary School :: Maple Grove

What I Hear in the Nighttime

When I'm awake in my bed I hear the
soft sound of a train whistle, be-e-e-e-e-e-p—
be-e-e-e-e-ep. I also hear the sound of deer
running through the forest like a bullet rushing
through the air. I also hear the soft sound
of the wind saying O-O-O-O-O-O-O-O. When
I'm awake in my bed I hear the sound of
trees swaying back and forth and when
I hear all that noise I get a warm feeling
in my heart that says, "It's a good world,
it's a good world."

Adam Schenk :: Grade 2
Gordon Bailey Elementary School :: Woodbury

Something to Love

Flowers blooming behind the bush
purple, pink and white.
Butterflies swarming all around
with cats close behind.
Friends sitting on the steps
watching the sunset droop.
Candles flaming on the ledge
red, orange and yellow.
Puppies sleeping in the basket
sweet, soft, and sound.

Carrie Tabery :: Grade 6
Wadena-Deer Creek Elementary School :: Deer Creek

THAT SUMMER

On those hot summer days
Cora and Amanda and I
Raced across our long yard.
After they left,
I played with Bella, my imaginary friend.
Then, it started to rain.
I used to think God poured water on you.
Soon, Mother called me in for supper,
And the crickets started chirping
"Chirp! Chirp!"
While I ate,
The rain leaped across the roof.
I saw the long strips of yellow lightning
Spread across the sky.
Maybe it would touch me, I thought.
Then dishes clattered together.
I went downstairs, then I ran up again.
I thought a monster was chasing me up.
It was only my vivid imagination.
After I went to bed,
I felt spiders crawling on my back.
I heard a rustling noise outside,
But I saw only shadows and blackness.
And now those summer days are gone!

Lisa Sahli :: Grade 4
J. F. Kennedy Elementary School :: Hastings

SHIRLEY

It was late in August, my brother, sister and I were having fun exploring our new house. We had just arrived at our new home late the night before, and so early in the morning we were up discovering like Christopher Columbus. My parents had moved into this house while we were visiting our grandparents in Idaho. They had settled in and met some of our new neighbors. One of those neighbors was Shirley.

I remember the morning that Shirley came over. She knocked on the door and when we opened it, a burst of sunshine rushed in. Shirley's hair was liquid sunshine and it was piled high on her head. She looked like a movie star from Hollywood because of her hair.

Shirley's face was sanguine but it was beautiful. The smile lines around her eyes and mouth showed off with pride. Her brilliant happiness, a joy from within. I also remember Shirley's eyes. They were playful, teasing and so full of life.

I was awestruck as I opened the door and let Shirley in. If she was nervous I couldn't tell, she was so bubbly and she seemed so tranquil, as if she'd known us forever. She brought us gifts and introduced us to her son. She smiled continuously and showed us nothing but gentle love and compassion. She didn't say very much, and what she did say I can't remember, but I knew she would play an important role in my life. This is the very first memory I have of Shirley.

I remember going to Shirley's house for the first time. My father told me that Shirley's house was beautiful on the inside and that it meant a lot to her. I was curious to see her house. I couldn't imagine what kind of house Shirley would live in.

The house was yellow then. The roof was harsh against the pastel fragility. Shirley's house reminded me of corn muffins spread thick with blackberry jam. Shirley opened the door. She did it how she did everything, with a smile. I saw behind her the vast white carpet, so soft and so perfect. I saw the deep wooden brown of the organ and the glossy shine of her wooden table.

I stepped into Shirley's house with great care, hoping I wouldn't disturb the splendor that her marvelous house had to offer. My second memory of Shirley is her house. Shirley and I have many other memories, some good, some of them not so good. One thing I do know, though. Shirley has played a major role in my life.

Holly Allen :: Grade 9
Prior Lake High School :: Prior Lake

PORK AND BEANS

When I was young
All I heard of him
Were stories of a great man.
He liked to make jokes
And he loved "pork and beans."
Every time I went to the store
I stopped,
The huge can of beans
In my hands.
"Look Mom,
Beans for Cal!"
When he was at our house
He asked,
"Got any beans?"
So I went and got
The biggest can we had.
The last time I saw him
He was cheery but thin.
He told about neighbors
Shooting off a potato gun
Hitting a stoplight
And it shattering.
He was still Cal
Now not too young
But still not older.
A great man
Who liked to make jokes
And loved "pork and beans."

Kathy Jo Maudal :: Grade 8
Battle Lake Public School :: Battle Lake

Our Inscriptions

Remember
> the age of our
> banana seat bikes?
> Through the forest of chirping birds
> and croaking frogs
> the backs of our shirts stained
> with the splattered mud of the trails.

Remember
> seeing garter snakes
> and grasshoppers
> basking in the summer heat on the
> hot asphalt?
> How we loved to bask in the sun.

Remember
> riding on the white lines
> in the middle of our country highways?
> Never once did we see a car.

Remember
> putting Jokers and Jacks
> in our spokes?
> You had the hearts, I had the
> clubs.

Remember
> when we ran away on our
> bikes?
> Just for a day, just for a lifetime.

Remember
> closing our eyes and
> riding no-handed down happy hill?
> We'd skid on some loose gravel
> and take a fall.

Those scrapes, those bruises,
now scars,
our inscriptions in stone.

Christopher Czyscon :: Grade 10
Elk River High School :: Elk River

THIS WAY

This is the way to sit up:
don't slouch

This is the way to walk:
don't skip.

These are the things you'll
need to know to become
an adult.

Come along now, this
way.

Don't pet that cat, it has
fleas.

Don't stare at people that way.

You'll never have respect
if you do those things
you do.

Come along now, this way.

This is the way to put out
a fire with a fire extinguisher.

This is the way to cut your bread
with a knife.

You must learn from me,
for your grandma is old.

Come along now, this way.

"No thank you, I
want to go out and play."

Becky Schultz :: Grade 6
Twin Bluff Middle School :: Red Wing

GIVE BACK HOPE TO THE OCEAN

TALK TO ME

There's all kind of talk that you hear around
All over the world people make that sound
English, French, babies make it too
"Hello," "Bonjour," and "Goo-Goo"
Quiet talk, loud talk, it's how we share
It's how we get from here to there

> Hello! Hello! Is anybody out there, I want to know?
> Hello! Hello! Please talk to me because I'm feeling low

You can talk about sports, you can talk about dogs
You can talk about cats, and the price of logs
Talk to your friends, you can talk to your brother
Even your sister, maybe your mother
Talk outside, talk in the hall
Sometimes you end up talking to the wall

(Chorus)

You can talk on the playground, and over at school
But not during reading, that's the rule
You can't talk when the baby's asleep
You'll wake her up, and make her weep
You can talk on vacation or at home
Especially when you are using the phone

(Chorus)

Ms. Johnson's Class :: Grade 3
Parkway Elementary School :: St. Paul

here to there. Hel - lo! _____ Hel - lo!

Is a - ny - bo - dy _____ out there I

want to know? _ Hel - lo! _____ Hel - lo!

Please talk to me be-cause I'm feel - ing low. _____

I need a dove
to cover my heart with peace.

A coat
to warm me up from bad things.

A pillow
to comfort me from the rough cold ground.

A window
to light up my life.

A door
to let things past me.

A tree
for me to climb up to see what is next.

A light socket
to charge up my life.

An animal
for me to talk to when I have problems.

A puzzle piece
to finish putting my life together.

A feather
to try to lift me up.

A map
to guide me to safety.

A spider web
to catch things I don't want near me.

A towel
to dry off my tears when I cry.

An eagle
to show me grace and beauty.

Rob Uebler :: Grade 5
Alice Smith Elementary School :: Hopkins

NEVER AGAIN

My great-aunt used
to be here but she passed
away one night. I'll never forget
the smell of dust and perfume,
the smell of hot, steaming gravy
in the kitchen. My great-aunt used
to give me a sucker every time
I went to her house. She always
had something to talk about,
something exciting. My aunt
was energetic as a
bolt of lightning. My great-aunt
meant as much to me as my
family does. She had a warm and welcoming
smile and her hands were soft
and smelled like lotion. She was never
too busy to play a game of cards,
or do something, anything with me.
My great-aunt was never harsh
or strict. Her house had rooms
with little surprises every time
you went into one. I never knew
my great-uncle because he also
passed away. Now I'm never going to
smell the hot, steaming gravy or the
old dust or perfume. I'll never again
see her warm welcoming smile or
feel her soft lotion-smelling hands.

I miss my aunt, I can never speak
to her again, never, never again.

Debbie Thiegs :: *Grade 4*
Gordon Bailey Elementary School :: *Woodbury*

HOLLOW

Hollow is a pain without feeling.
Hollow is a wall that is invisible.
Hollow is a magnet that doesn't stick.
Hollow is a pregnant stomach without a baby inside.
Hollow is a fish that you can see through.
Hollow is taking a shower without any water.

Thida Nop :: Grade 4
Parkway Elementary School :: St. Paul

WHEN MY DAD DIED

This picture is about
when my dad
died. I
was sad. I
think this picture
is here so I
will always remember.
All the trees
are dead because
they are sad too.

When I looked into his eyes I saw
the sun, when I
held his hand I
felt a spirit, when
I go to sleep I
see him far
far away.
I will follow his
footsteps.

Curtis Hanson :: Grade 5
Ames Elementary School :: St. Paul

Falling, Falling, Falling

I have a dream and all
I'm doing is falling,
falling, falling.

Is it the emptiness in
me that's falling, falling,
        falling?

Is it the hope being
shattered that's falling,
falling, falling?

Am I alone and the loneliness
in me is falling, falling,
        falling.

Is it a part of my heart
that's falling, falling, falling?

Is it just me that's falling,
falling, falling?

Is it just soaring like a bird
only to know I'm
        falling, falling, falling?

Is it the hole left in me
from the people who left me
that's falling, falling, falling?

Will I ever stop falling, falling,
        falling?

Am I going to fall like a
drop of rain in the sky
only to keep falling, falling,
        falling . . .

'Til I die?

Rachel Connelly :: Grade 7
Oltman Junior High School :: St. Paul Park

UNTITLED

I lay on the couch
wrapped in thirty dollars of Telfa Non-
Stick pads and Sterile Gauze like a mummy
lying in his coffin. My boxers
sticking out of my sagging shorts.
The smell of burnt flesh still lingers
in my nose. I was watching movies
because my singed hands could not support
a book. The room swaying a bit
from the codeine. Then he came in.
"Hey, Man, how's it going!"
He smelled distinctly of McDonalds.
My stomach churned at the smell.
It couldn't keep a prisoner for two days.
My ribs were exposed even
through the bandages. He said, "Smile!"
My lip turned up, the chasm in my
cheek opened, a row of white teeth
marched to the forefront to be
captured by the eternities. Oh, how my
mouth craved the special sauce, and my
belly rejected the thought. My body, still
scarred, the pain and anger live
in my mind. Why me?

Kenyon Hoyt :: Grade 11
Stillwater High School :: Stillwater

TRAPPED

I am the river with nowhere to run,
your room when parents are mad.
I am the cell that prisoners sit in,
a room at a mental hospital.
I am the pound where your lost dog sits,
the lion locked in the cage
that everyone stares at.
I am your gold fish in your fish bowl
or the cage in which the bird sings.
I am the character in the book
that no one wants to read.
I am a maze with no way out.

Jeannette LaFavor :: Grade 12
Alternative Learning Center :: St. Paul Park

I walk the path
my feet are bricks of stone.

I shuffle along,
kicking up dirt as I go.

My head pounds like Zeus',
my heart beats, I have no doubt it will burst.

The path is as long
as Picard's on the USS Enterprise.

I see a light,
and it gives me strength.

I reach the light,
a small lantern over the door of an inn.

I try the door,
the handle is cold, wet.

The door is locked,
the inn empty.

Jolanta N. Komornicka :: Grade 6
St. Rose of Lima School :: Roseville

AFTERNOON CRUSH

Every time I smell mothballs, it's 1989.
I find myself hunched over beneath
the top bunk in my room at Camp Galilee.
My bare feet have settled onto the cold
cement floor, and my eyes onto the wooden
panel of the bunk across from mine.

The brown paisley curtains hesitate
as the warm summer breeze wanders
in through the screen. For a moment
the room lights up. Then again, it's dark.
They call it quiet time. Everyone in the dorm
is resting. Except me.

Once more my eyes fall onto the written
tales of the past, carelessly scribbled
into a surface of pine.
I see her name there, but not mine.

Emptiness leaps
from the wooden plank into the depths
of my heart.
Underneath
sheets of compassion
I cry.

Jeremy Erickson :: Grade 12
Roseau High School :: Roseau

TRUCK DRIVER GOING DOWN STEEP HILL

Fear, there is none here, only a broken
heart for those back home: sleepiness, only
I know what it is like to drive all
day and all night. I feel every
journey I take inside me: Steep
cliffs that drop straight down and fear
of falling to what could be endless
death. Worry of what would become of
loved ones back home. As you are slipping
your life is on hold, for what seems
to be days. Wondering if what people say
is true, that right before you die your life
flashes before your eyes. Life is
an endless journey.

Joe Borash :: Grade 9
Holdingford High School :: Holdingford

SCENE: The sun is shining. GRANDPA is on stage. His beard is very long: down to the ground. The BEARD is played by several actors who tangle themselves around each other. The GIRL stands on the other side of the stage from GRANDPA.

THE SUN: What a beautiful day!

[The CAT enters. It goes to the GIRL. But before it gets there, GRANDPA's BEARD grows fast and wraps around the CAT. The CAT is pulled down into the BEARD.]

CAT: Meowwwwwwww.

[The BROTHER enters. The BEARD grows all around him and pulls him down.]

BROTHER: Ahhhhhh . . .

[The MOM enters. She trips on something in the BEARD (the CAT), falls, and disappears into GRANDPA'S BEARD.]

MOM: Ahhhhhh . . .

[The BEARD grows up around the GIRL. It pulls her down into itself.]

GIRL: Ahhh . . .

[A pause.]

THE SUN: What a beautiful day.

GRANDPA: Shut up. It is not.

THE SUN: What a beautiful day.

GRANDPA: I told you shut up. It is not a beautiful day.

[A MYSTERIOUS STRANGER enters. She carries a pair of scissors. She snips off GRANDPA's BEARD, right by his face. The BEARD falls off of everyone, and the CAT, the BROTH-ER, MOM, and the GIRL all stand up, relieved.]

THE SUN: What a beautiful day.

[Suddenly GRANDPA's BEARD grows fast again, grabbing everyone and pulling them down again. As the GIRL sinks into the BEARD, she says:]

GIRL: We're never inviting you over again!

Rachel Kilau :: Grade 3
Pullman Elementary School :: St. Paul Park

THE HOODS

My cousins and I were hanging around dancing, watching people get jumped. I'm wearing purple, Joni is wearing white and Robin is wearing black. We went in the house to get some money from my grandma, and then we walked to the store. When we got there, there was a stick-up by a man who had just gotten out of jail. Me and my cousins were just sitting there looking at the magazines until we heard a gunshot. We were out, you didn't see us at that store no more.

The next day we were walking down the street and a gang started running after us. My cousin got in deep trouble, Robin got jumped. When we got to the beauty parlor we called the police. That gang was put in prison for two years.

Later, when they got out, we moved to a better side of town. My mom's dad had died. My cousins Joni and Robin and my aunt said that I could go live with them. I did, so that my Mom had time to think things out on where else we were going to live, when we were going to move, how we were going to move. I was mad because my family was there in Chicago.

I never thought it would be that way, so we got to stay and I was so happy. We kept on riding our bikes, letting the wind blow through the air, and never forgetting the time we saw Snoop Doggy Dog when we were little.

We are twelve now, and so that was three years ago. That was the past. Now my family is living large, happy, and on the south side of Chicago. Nothing else could bother us again.

Unless . . .

April Guy :: Grade 6
Grant Magnet School :: Duluth

SCENE: A BOY on the way to his tree house.

BOY: I feel like someone is watching me.

[He walks some more.]

BOY: I really feel like someone is watching me.

[He gets to his tree house, climbs up in it. Wind begins to blow. The tree shakes. Scary music plays. The SUN (played by several people in a clump making burning noises) comes out of the sky, and tries to burn the BOY in the tree house. On the way to the BOY the SUN lights a giant MATCH, which lights a giant CIGAR. The BOY jumps out of the tree house just as the SUN crashes into the tree. The tree burns down. The giant MATCH and the giant CIGAR surround the BOY, puffing smoke on him and trying to burn him. He dodges them. A big headed GREEN THING enters and goes towards the BOY.]

GREEN THING: LUNCH TIME!!!!!!

[The BOY runs away, but is stopped by a giant HAWK, who screeches at him and chases him back toward the GREEN THING. The BOY transforms into a tank. He does this by squatting down and sticking out his arms like the barrel of the gun. He fires at the GREEN THING. But the HAWK comes between him and the GREEN THING. The HAWK swallows all the cannon balls.]

BOY: I hate that bird!

[The giant MATCH tries to burn the BOY. The BOY produces a hose to squirt water on the MATCH. Again, the HAWK comes in between the BOY and the MATCH. The HAWK swallows all the water.]

BOY: I hate that bird!!

[The MATCH, the GREEN THING, and the CIGAR back away. The SUN comes in, heading for the BOY. Just before the

BOY is burnt up by the SUN, the HAWK comes in between them. The SUN stops.]

THE SUN: Dang it! Dang it! Dang it!!

[The SUN backs away.]

The HAWK: (to the BOY:) All bad things come to an end.

[The HAWK flies off, waving good bye to the BOY.]

Nick Swanlund :: Grade 4
Pullman Elementary School :: St. Paul Park

DAN

Fill my heart with eagles so I can live,
Give back hope to the ocean.
Let me soar with freedom,
Let me wander around the world.
Without my soul I have no feeling,
Give me back my heart so I can love again.
I'm confused without your guidance,
Guide me to the end of the world.

Dan Kreuser :: Grade 6
Pine Hill Elementary School :: Cottage Grove

FLYING EAGLE

A poem is like an eagle flying high,
no limits or boundaries.
It's smooth and shiny like the bald head.
It has beautiful rhythm
like the coal-colored feathers.

It's hard to catch a poem.
It's as evasive as the eagle.
You have to watch and listen to the poem
or you might become its prey.

A poem stands alone on a cliff.
It watches over and laughs at us
for trying to figure it out.

Poem—is there really a meaning?
Who cares, just listen to the beauty
and enjoy the peace.
Let the poem fly high and glide.
Just as the eagle,
never limit its spacious sky!

Chad Pothen :: Grade 9
KMS High School :: Kerkhoven

Being the Wind

being the wind
is like seeing an earth spin by you,
like not feeling the wind
but feeling the still air instead

because I am the wind

I hear the trees say
slow down
as I rush past them

I should know, I am the wind

I hear the hang gliders say
faster, faster

I should know, I am the wind

my life is short though,
I start in the heavens
and race to the earth,
where I die and float
up to the heavens and do it again

because I am the wind, I should know . . .

Geoffrey Boeder :: Grade 5
Tanglen Elementary School :: Hopkins

NATURE'S POWER

As dusk quietly inhabits the sky,
the harsh night wind blows the fallen leaves.
Time stands still, though only for a moment.
My eyes glance at the radiant stars
while the golden moon cowardly hides behind a large
     gray cloud.

The moment of silence is disrupted by a sudden crash
     of thunder,
and the ebony sky opens to a streak of deadly silver
     lightning.

The howling wind rapidly picks up speed,
as the once friendly blue clouds wrap around the
     entire sky
hiding all that's behind them with their massive gray
     bodies.

Sheets of glistening rain drop consistently upon the
     awaiting ground.
Nature is demonstrating its power to all who want to
     see.

Janel Dopheide :: Grade 9
Worthington Area Junior High School :: Worthington

THE STORM

I am a cardinal
I am making my loud majestic call
I wear a gorgeous red crown
I am swiftly flying through
the oil black sky
trying to override the storm

Joseph Masrud :: Grade 3
Webster Magnet School :: St. Paul

The lightning splits
an oak tree in half
says the lion
on his hunt.
The sunlight skims through
the trees in the yard,
says the crow
in the air.
The northern light
splits the southern stars
says the ocean
in the west.
The fire spreads fast
in the meadow
says the frightened panther.
The reflection in the river
follows me,
says the swimming fish.

Cory Knight :: Grade 5
Glen Lake Elementary School :: Hopkins

STARS

The stars sail across the sky
Like a baby's mobile across the crib,
Moving with the wind.
The stars delight all: men, women, children.

The stars sail across the sky
As a boat does through dark endless waters.
The people aboard the boat are singing
And working to the light of the stars.

The stars sail across the sky
Like children playing ring-around-the-rosies
But the stars rarely fall, unlike
The sweet children of our earth.

The stars sail across the sky
Like dancing butterflies, leaping ballet dancers.
They twinkle and shine
Until the rising sun puts their fun to an end.

Jessica Cohen :: Grade 7
St. Paul Academy :: St. Paul

BOBCAT

Bobcat, royal cat, do you still sniff
the flowers like we used to?
Do you still think of yourself as
a rabbit being able to jump so far?
Do you still see the darkness that roams
in you? Do you still see the tree that
you lay under for shade? How about
the lion that is hunting and is ready
to eat? Do you still smell the
honey falling from the tree two
miles away? When you find your
prey, do you still smell the fear
that it gives off? Can you
still hear the leaves fall that land
on the soil that you lay on? When
we would smell the flowers, do you
still hear the wind going through
them? Do you hear your blood moving
through your heart? Do you hear
the eagle as it swoops down
to find its prey? When we used
to smell the flowers, do you still
feel the pollen on your nose? What about
the soft grass as it
touches your paws? Do you feel
the soft petting I used to give you?
What about the honey? Do you
still taste the warm honey as
it trickles down your throat? Bobcat,
royal cat, how are you?

Rachelle Engelking :: *Grade 5*
Hillside Elementary School :: *Cottage Grove*

A TALE

Once upon a time there was a boy who loved to play with animals. This boy's name was Wonyama.

Wonyama was a nice boy who always understood what the animals were trying to tell him. One day a baby elephant came to him and said, "Help, help! Someone is shooting my mother."

So Wonyama followed the baby elephant into the forest to where the mama elephant was shot and killed. Wonyama took the baby elephant home to live with him.

When the boy got home to his mother, she said, "No way, boy, are you keeping that *thang* in my house."

And the boy said, "Please Mama, I'll take care of this little elephant."

"Well, I guess so," said Mama.

And the little elephant lived with Wonyama for a long time. But one day the elephant grew to be very big, and had to move away. And have a family of his own.

Brandon Simiyu :: Grade 6
Nettleton Magnet School :: Duluth

Jenny was riding Buster, a spirited black horse that gets moody or cranky. Right then he was cantering across the fields. All of a sudden Buster's attitude changed.

"What's the matter, Buster?" Jenny asked.

Then Buster stopped cantering and his ears lay flat back.

"Come on, boy. What's wrong? You were doing great."

Then he started to buck. Jenny hung on, but after he had stopped Jenny relaxed. Then he bucked one last time, hard!

Jenny flew off the saddle. Everything seemed to be going in slow motion for a few seconds. Jenny could see the land coming closer and closer. All of a sudden Jenny landed HARD on her stomach.

She sat there for a few seconds. Jenny had got the wind knocked out of her. Then when she got her breath back, Jenny looked where Buster had gone. Luckily, he was only ten feet away.

Jenny pulled herself up so she was standing. Jenny started to walk towards him but he laid his ears back. Jenny said, "Buster, it's okay. I'm not mad at you. You probably just got confused or scared. It's okay."

When his ears popped up, Jenny started walking toward him and mounted him. He was perfect,

"That's my boy," Jenny said lovingly.

After about a half hour Jenny brought him back to the stables and groomed him. When she was picking his hooves, she found a rock in his foot. She got that out and he was one of the best horses she had ever ridden from then on. They were the best of friends after that.

Maria Cates :: Grade 6
St. John the Baptist School :: Excelsior

My Red Rock

My rock looks like
fire, but on the other
side it looks like a
fire that is just starting.
My rock is rough. It
reminds me of a red
rose that grows in
the ground. The End
of the rock story:
good-bye fire red rose.

Rachel Hugley :: Grade 1
Homecroft Elementary School :: St. Paul

BLUE

Blue is for the echo of the waves crashing into the rocks that line the shore. Blue is for the deep heart-driven sadness that reaches us when we are in the blues. It is for the gecko who crawls on the ground and is alert for predators in the warmth. It is for the sky's wonder, and the blue jay's calls. Blue is for the exotic birds that live scattered all around the tropical heat of the forest. Blue is for the hippo's laziness, as it sits in the mudhole, its skin shining in the hot African sun. Blue is for our nation, hanging on the flag guarding us. It is for the eyes of a bride being wedded into marriage. Blue is the sweet taste of blueberries on a hot summer day, refreshing and great. Blue is someone's cheeks as they swim through the deep water as they hold their breath intensely, not like the envied fish around. It is for the unforgettable lake's beauty, shining and shimmering in the sun's arms. It's for the peregrine falcon's grace as it flies overhead, swooping down steeply as if to greet you. It is for the sorrowful rain that sprinkles down onto the ground with peaceful plops. Blue is for the bluebird's caws as it flies over your head, and you envy its flight. Blue is for the spread of joy, may we all have it in our hearts forever.

Steven P. Pope :: Grade 5
St. Michael-Albertville Elementary School :: St. Michael

WORLD OF COLORS

Happiness to the butterfly
who hops from colored rose
to colored rose, red, blue
and yellow. Joy to the sea
where fish swim and
jump in schools, red, blue,
purple and yellow.
Gladness to the fog who
makes the world gray and misty.

Paul Robert Jonas :: Grade 1
Parkway Elementary School :: St. Paul

UNTITLED

Why doesn't the mole come out
of his little hole? He's a funny
little animal, that funny little
mole.
Who dug up the dinosaurs from
their giant graves? It would
be fun again, but they'd
have to be caged.
Why do flowers
grow from their little seeds? They
grow very pretty and they seem all for me.

Donovan Thorgrimson :: Grade 1
Aquila Primary Center :: St. Louis Park

SMELL OF ROSES

Roses smell like perfume
on a woman.
They smell good
on a summer day.
They smell like dirt
on a spring year.
The roses smell like
the Holy Spirit.

Lloyd Pugh :: Grade 7
Le Sueur-Henderson Junior High School :: Le Sueur

TREE

Tree, tree, you're so green.
Tree, tree, with a snake in it
and the snake got the bird's nest
in the tree for a home.
Tree, tree, the trunk so brown.
Tree, tree, with the owl living in it.
Tree, tree, I'm climbing up the tree.
Tree, tree with a hundred rings.
Tree, tree, with the lumberjacks
cutting you down.
Tree, tree, you're so green.

Christopher Luedemann :: Kindergarten
(assisted by Andy Garten :: Grade 6)
Fernbrook Elementary School :: Maple Grove

Winter/Spring

Winter sky is snowy and cold
And it's colored white
The spring sky is blue and warm
And you can fly a kite

Winter ground is covered up
Covered up with snow
Spring ground is covered with sun
The trees begin to grow

Winter water looks like glass
Sparkly and clear
Spring water is warm and wet
And good for the deer

Ms. Ylonen's, Ms. Johnson's and Ms. Lundquist's classes :: Kindergarten
Parkway Elementary School :: St. Paul

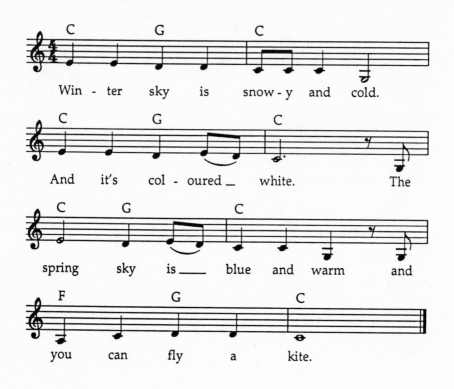

WATERFALL

My waterfall
mysteriously beautiful
as it races from the high
rocky place above.
Farther behind the waterfall,
I am awestruck
by the burst
of a strong misty smell
coming at me.
Past the everlasting flow of water,
I see beautiful icicles
that take centuries
of years to form.
I touch the rough
rugged walls of my cave,
my cave of mysterious icicles.
Hearing a loud rush of water,
I'm taken back
by everything I'll ever
see there.
My waterfall,
the cave of mystery.

Kelly Peters :: Grade 5
Gatewood Elementary School :: Hopkins

WHALES DREAM

It was the dream of the whale,
Who swims in the shallow pool
As he circles his own path,
Wishing for a fresh, deep breath.

His eyes, like brilliant stars
Falling from the top of a mountain,
Stunning every living soul.
A giant kite
Flying through the midnight sky,
In his tail.
His skin, the shining image of sheer silk.
A screech, like the moan of two mice
Scampering from the hungry eagle
When it glides through the dark.
As the whale flies
Through the shadowed blue water,
He makes the seashore tremble with jealousy.

Yet, he was brought forth
From the sweeping and gliding wind's realm,
And the gentle, yet daring features
Of a rose petal falling to its eternal death.

Sara Polley :: Grade 5
Greenleaf Elementary School :: Apple Valley

The Hawk in Me

When I was a hawk, I could see a jungle
with lions, tigers and birds. I could
see rolling mountains. I could
hear a lion getting his prey. I
heard an owl landing in its house.
I heard a squirrel screaming
to another. I used to fly up and spot
a salmon. I could smell fruit far
away. I could feel the coldness
of tomorrow. I could hear the stream
talking to the fish in a low whisper.
The trout tasted like chicken to a
hawk like me. I used to dive into a
lake to cool off. Life to a hawk is
like life now. I felt I could fly to
the next country, that is how happy
I was when I was a hawk. When I was a
hawk, I could do anything.

Nick Bad Heart Bull :: Grade 4
Holdingford Elementary School :: Holdingford

The Earth's Laugh

Hear the heart pound
against the Earth's floor!
As it laughs around the sun,
Earth moves.
Look at it dance
around the sun!
Earth started laughing
at its dancing.
Can you hear it?
It laughs around you!
Hear the heart pound!
The wind will
blow you away with
the sounds of Earth's laugh!

Teresa Dondelinger :: Grade 6
Central Middle School :: Columbia Heights

TELL ME A STORY,
TAKE ME AWAY

Tell Me A Story

Tell me a story, take me away
At night, or any time of the day
Talk with me, sing to me, dance for me too
Tell me a story please do, please do
Tell me a story please do

Take me to a forest, with big green trees
Or to castles, with kings and queens
It's so exciting and mysterious too
Tell me a story please do, please do
Tell me a story, please do

Take me to places far under the sea
With mermaids and dolphins how fun it would be
It's a journey with family and friends just like you
Tell me a story please do, please do
Tell me a story please do

Make me an astronaut or a captain on deck
Shock me, surprise me, scare me like heck
Read me a mystery, show me a clue
Tell me a story please do, please do
Tell me a story please do

Ms. Mahon's Class :: Grade 3
St. Francis Xavier School :: Buffalo

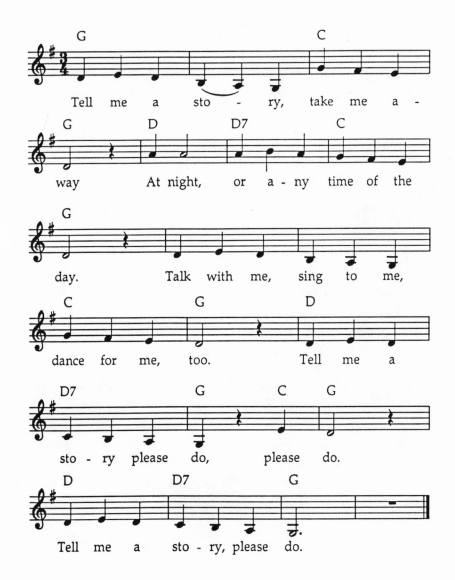

DINO BONES

I woke up at 8:30 on the dot one Saturday morning. I'm Carly Hoch. I am a dino-bone-digger. I got out of my warm bed, got dressed and went downstairs. I was greeted by the smell of cinnamon rolls and bacon. The scent led me downstairs and into the kitchen. On the counter was a stack of mail. I looked through it. Bills, bills, bills. (Those are for my mom.) One more bill and a letter for me. I took it and read it. It said:

Miss Carly N. Hoch,

We understand you are a bone-digger. We have a job for you in Billings, Montana. Come ASAP.

Sincerely,

National Museum of Dinos
Billings, Montana

I was overjoyed! A job! At last! I packed my bags immediately. I couldn't drive yet, and I knew my mom wouldn't drive me all the way to Montana (we live in Wyoming), so I decided I'd have to walk. I left a note for mom and started off.

I saw some bright red cardinals in the trees. It felt wonderful to have a job at last, and in beautiful Montana! The dew on the grass was soaking my shoes, so I slipped them off. I ran alongside the road for a while until I got hungry. I pulled a big apple out of my bag. I took a huge bite. Yum! A juicy, sweet, and slightly tangy apple. Everything seemed to be so perfect today. I saw a stand up ahead. I walked closer. I was in luck! A map stand. I had no idea where I was going anyway. There was a tall, thin man at the counter. He had a slight beginning of a moustache.

"What kind of map do ya want?" he asked when I walked up. He had a scratchy voice.

"Um . . ." I stammered. "I . . . I really don't know what kind of maps you have, sir."

"What?" he screeched. "What kind of maps do you think I have!"

I shrank back. I was tempted to run away, but remembering my job I planted both feet on the ground. "Okay, I'd like one of the USA," I said quietly.

"Where yer folks, hot dog?" he asked, eyeing me.

"Ah . . ." I had to think fast. "Um . . . they're at home. I mean, they were at home. They should be coming along any time now."

I grabbed the map, paid fifty cents, and ran out as fast as I could. I looked at the map. Oh, boy! I was less than ten miles away! I walked slowly so I wouldn't waste my energy. One and one-half hour later, I saw a big brown sign that said:

WELCOME TO BILLINGS, MONT!

population: 45,000

I was there at last! Up ahead was a big yellow building with a sign that said: National Museum of Dinos. I practically skipped inside the building. It smelled of floor wax. I almost slid to the manager's office. I opened the door. Inside I saw a big bulky man with glasses that looked ten times too big for him. A smelly cigar hung out of his mouth.

"Carly Hoch, I presume," he said in a deep, rumbling voice.

"Yes," I squeaked. He was kind of scary. I closed the door behind me.

"Where are your folks?" he asked.

I just couldn't lie again. It would make things too complicated. I sighed. "They didn't come. I'm here alone." I kind of felt weak.

"Well, then, I can't take you for the job. I need your parents to sign these papers."

By now my knees felt like jelly. I had to sit down.

"Please call your mother to take you home," he boomed, pointing to a big red phone.

So I did. I got grounded for two weeks, but there would be other jobs, hopefully on my block.

Carly Hoch :: Grade 4
Fernbrook Elementary School :: Maple Grove

The alligator has a tale:

One day the giraffe who lived in the water was having fun in the water. But then he bent his long neck and sat on his head.

The tiger named Duck asked, "Why did he sit on his head?"

The elephant can't remember her name. She asked, "If I can't remember my name, how would I know why he sat on his head?"

The bird was going on a trip. The bird said, "I don't care why he sat on his head. I'm taking a vacation to Arkansas."

Crystal, the zebra, was playing dice and flew away. She didn't care why the giraffe sat on his head. The lion was eating fish and he didn't care why the giraffe sat on his head. The panda was only a toy so he didn't know why the giraffe was sitting on his head.

But the monkey loved God. He said, "The giraffe is sitting on his head because he was praying."

Mr. Hallman's Class :: Grade 2
Parkway Elementary School :: St. Paul

One of the kids yelled, "We want a story!"

"All right, all right," I said. I'll tell you the story of your great, great-great-great-great-great-grandfather Treo."

A long time ago in the time of wizards, warlocks and knights, one of our ancestors was a ranger, because back then they didn't have policemen. One day when he was in a tavern he heard about a treasure.

"Yep, there's treasure in that cavern on Willow Hill," said the drunken man who just passed out into a bowl of soup.

Treo made plans that day to go to the cavern. When he was buying supplies a man came up and said, "I'm coming, too."

Treo found himself looking into two eyes which were brown. Treo just looked and there stood a two-storey red dragon.

"What's wrong?"

Treo couldn't believe his eyes. I mean, there stood a dragon with blood red scales and he asked him what was wrong.

"Y-y-y-you're a dragon!" Treo half-mumbled.

"Oh, I'm sorry," and then he turned into a wizard.

They talked for a while with Treo still baffled. They agreed that they would split the treasure in half.

The next day they went up to the spot and they saw a big hole. They went down and it opened up to a big open chamber and little passages leading off.

The wizard cast a spell which gave him the ability to see through walls, but little did they know they were being watched.

They wound through a maze of passages. Then after a long while there was a long, long corridor and it smelled gross.

Then Treo knew why it smelled so bad. Then Treo shouted, "DUCK!"

The wizard turned to see what was happening and Treo leaped and shoved the wizard down. Just then a gust of flame came out of the wall.

The wizard said, "How did you know?"

"I smelt oil," explained Treo.

Then they started hacking on the wall and after a while they came to a secret passage. They got in and someone said, "What are you doing in my cave?"

The wizard cast a spell that made a shield for him that was like a jail.

The man yelled, "Get me out of here!"

All of a sudden men, probably servants, came up and surrounded them and knocked them out cold.

They awoke in a small chamber. It was stone all around. Then a voice said, "Pass these tests and you may have the treasure." The cell door opened and he said, "Light is the key that opens possibility." There was only a mirror, a door and some light shining down from the ceiling. Then Treo got it.

He grabbed the mirror and reflected it at the keyhole of the door. Then came a loud click and the door swung open.

The next room had some water dripping from glistening stalactites. But just then a balisk came from the darkness and used its deadly gaze to turn the wizard into stone.

Treo closed his eyes and ran towards the balisk with his mirror facing the balisk. The balisk tried to turn him into stone but the gaze hit the mirror and turned him into stone instead. A few minutes after he was turned to stone, he shrunk into a man; in fact, the same man who had told his servants to attack Treo and the wizard. The wizard was unstoned because the balisk was defeated. Then the next door opened and there was the treasure—a whole room filled with gold coins!

"There, did you like the story?"

Robby Henderson :: Grade 4
Fernbrook Elementary School :: Maple Grove

THE EARTH AND THE ANTS

When people litter the earth feels angry.
The fish cry. The apple trees stomp.
All the apples growl.
The clouds hit the mountain.
When people clean up, the earth feels happy.
Ants come out and shout, "Yea!"
They jump in the puddle and swim all the way across.
The earth laughs at the ants.

Mallory Bernardson :: Grade 1
Fernbrook Elementary School :: Maple Grove

IF I WERE TEENY TINY

If I were teeny tiny,
if I were teeny tiny,
I would live in a doll house
or a birdhouse made out of match sticks.
I'd ride a beetle, a toy car,
and on the end of a dog's tail.

If I were teeny tiny,
If I were teeny tiny,
I'd sleep in a bed of cotton balls
with beans or a strawberry for a pillow.
I'd use a leaf for a blanket
and sleep in a mouse hole.

If I were teeny tiny,
if I were teeny tiny,
I'd buy clothes at the doll shop
and find a sewing pin to make a mouse suit.
I'd jump into the sink, take a bath,
and use a dime for a surfboard.

If I were teeny tiny,
if I were teeny tiny,
I'd fly on a paper airplane
and swim in a little cup or a fish tank.
I'd twirl around on a mobile or a fan
and jump into a chocolate cake.

If I were teeny tiny,
if I were teeny tiny,
I'd make a snowman out of mint ice cream.
I'd climb on my aunt's slipper
and tickle the bottom of her foot.

Mr. Schak's and Ms. Strong's Classes :: Kindergarten
North End Elementary School :: St. Paul

"Hello, Mouser! The hayloft is bigger and a whole lot softer, isn't it, Mouser?"

"Puzzles. Milk!"

"That's me," I thought. "Lunch time. Let's go!" Carrying Mouser, I ran down the hay and out the barn door and standing there was grumpy old Mrs. Cluck with her family of five. She gave a little grunt and put her nose up. Green light, I ran to the front porch and there was my warm milk with my favorite person, six-year-old Maria.

"Here you go, Puzzles. Your milk is warm and ready."

"Bye, Mouser!" I put Mouser down with a thud and gulped down my milk out of my "My Cat Dish" bowl. I licked all sides and jumped into Maria's arms. "Whoops," I thought. I licked Maria's face and picked up Mouser and went through the kitty door. Boy, was that a mistake. Inside I found a hairy blur of fur that was bigger than me. Its eyes were dark brown and when it saw me it gave a bark and a yipper. He, she, it jumped around like a mad dog and that's what it was—a mad dog named Squirt! Yikes! That wasn't enough.

"Here comes Mr. Thatcher with the seeds," yelled Peter. Mr. Thatcher, that mean old man. I made a dash for Mouser, who I had dropped, and headed past Squirt, who ran after me. My white little paws sprang out the kitty door and I took one paw forward, then the other, but then Mrs. Cluck ran in front of me trying to get out of the way of Mr. Thatcher's horse. The next thing I knew I was on my back looking up at a drooling and panting Squirt. Mouser was still in my mouth, but full of Squirt's slobber. I got up and saw four legs, tall ones, and they belonged to a horse. On that horse was a man with red, blazing eyes and with his nostrils flaring. I could tell Mr. Thatcher got off the wrong side of bed that morning. Yelling, he said, "Out of my way, you filthy brat of a cat!" With that his whip rose. His arm went up and then down and down. I closed my eyes and felt my collar being pulled.

I heard a snap of the whip, but I didn't feel it. I was being dragged, with Mouser in my mouth. I opened my eyes and saw Mr. Thatcher going farther and farther back. I felt Maria pick me up and comfort me. I looked down at Squirt and knew he saved me. I gave him a wink; at least I tried to (cats can't wink, you know). I knew he understood.

Sarah Greninger :: Grade 5
Fernbrook Elementary School :: Maple Grove

Once a girl named Clair was walking down the street. She was thinking about a problem. Her problem was her house was haunted. Something spooky was always happening. Last week, she found a secret note on her mirror.

She walked back to her house. There was a ghost on the porch. She thought it was her mom. She walked up to the porch. The ghost said, "Hello." Clair got up off the dirt, brushed off her knee, and ran to her best friend's house.

"Laura," said Clair. "My house is haunted. Help!"

"What?" said Laura.

Clair shouted again, "MY HOUSE IS HAUNTED!"

"Oh," said Laura.

Clair took Laura to her house.

Laura said, "Guess what your ghost is? It's a stuffed scarecrow!"

"What!" said Clair.

Laura said, "Your brother was probably playing a trick on you."

"What about the mirror message?" asked Clair.

"I left that," reminded Laura. "Remember, I came over last week and played haunted house."

Then Laura and Clair went and slept at Clair's house, and when they got up they told each other their dreams. They found they had had the same dream.

"Oh, no!" they exclaimed. "How did this happen?"

"Clair," said Laura, "I'm scared."

"Let's go see Mary," suggested Clair.

"OK," said Laura. Mary was at Carly's house across the street.

"Hi," Clair said. Mary and Carly ran over to them.

"Hey," exclaimed Mary, "what are you doing here?"

"I want you to come to my house," said Clair. When they got there, Clair told them that it really didn't happen, but just then the ghost reappeared on the porch.

"HELP!! LET'S GET OUT OF HERE!!" they all yelled.

"I don't think my brother was playing a trick on us! MY HOUSE IS HAUNTED!"

When they thought they were far enough away from Clair's

house, they sat down and Clair said, "I wonder if this ghost is a porch haunter?"

"Maybe," said a mysterious voice. They turned around and there was the ghost!!!!!

"OH, NO!!!" they all exclaimed at the same time. "What are we going to do?"

"Wait," exclaimed Clair. "My great-aunt Debbie died in my house and that ghost looks just like her.

"Ohoooo!" said Carly. "We are being haunted by your AUNT!"

"See," said Clair, "my aunt died when my mom was pregnant with me. She always wanted to meet me, but of course she never did. Now I think she came back to haunt me."

"Oh, no!" said Mary.

YOU'RE GOING TO HAVE TO WAIT FOR THE SEQUEL.

Amanda Nelson :: Grade 3
Aquila Primary Center :: St. Louis Park

Long ago the rivers and lakes always had water, and the soil was always moist, although it never rained.

One summer, an especially nice one, the people were having a good hunt. But when they went to hunt buffalo so they could dry the meat for winter, they didn't get a single one. All the people were very sad. That seemed to be the end of hunting, for none of the hunters could catch any game.

Ooleowo, the shaman, decided that he was going to figure out why this had happened. Surely there was a reason! There was always a reason for everything.

Ooleowo went out into the wilderness, searching for a reason. He saw a tree and high above it, among its branches, was a comfortable place to sit. Ooleowo climbed the tree, went into the place that he had seen from the ground, and fell asleep.

He dreamed that he was sitting in the tree watching Ohiyena and Laseuro, two young men from the village, who were off on a hunting trip. Both were good hunters. They were eating their evening meal and when they finished, they started painting their faces as if for a big dance. Laseuro finished first, and started dancing wildly around the fire while singing a hideous song. He sang about how lazy the god of rivers and lakes was, for Laseuro was a bad swimmer.

As he sang, he cursed, "You are guilty of the deaths of many brave people, and you almost killed me today, too. So I hope your rivers and lakes dry up!"

When Laseuro was done, Ohiyena got up and danced even wilder, he sang even wilder. "You god of hunting, you are so terrible at your job!" He half sang, half cried out. "You should let the people get meat whenever we need it! It would stop a lot of suffering! I curse you!"

When Ooleowo woke up, he climbed down the tree and looked around. And, exactly where he had seen fire in his dream, there were a few black coals left.

He went back to the village to tell the rest of the people. The people decided to form a council; and at the council meeting they decided that the two young warriors would have to sacrifice their dearest possessions, whatever they may be. The sacrificial ceremony was to be held the next day.

The next morning, when the council members went to find Ohiyena and Laseuro, they were not in their lodges. Tracks in the ground showed that they had crept out of the village during the night.

Scouts were sent out to look for Ohiyena and Laseuro, but no one was able to find them. All the scouts came back to the village, raging, "There are no signs of them anywhere!"

The village was filled with the sounds of wailing women; and men's angry voices shouted, "They had no right to do that to us! The cowards!"

The villagers tried to continue living as usual. But with the water level of the lakes and rivers going down, wild game was scarce as was plant growth. Discouraged hunters came home with no meat for their hungry families. And women spent fruitless days in search of roots and berries. Life was frequently interrupted by illness, especially among the youngest and the oldest, who were most vulnerable.

Ooleowo decided to do something about the situation. He went to the mountains, climbed a very high summit, and started chanting in a language only shamans and high animals knew. "Someone, come help my people! We are starving!"

Eagle heard Ooleowo's chanting and came to see what was the matter.

"The game is scarce," cried Ooleowo. "Plants are drying up and the water level of the rivers and lakes is going down. Please help in some way!"

Eagle answered, "I'll have to make the greatest flight I have ever made and consult Great Spirit as to what can be done."

"I wish you luck!" said Ooleowo.

Eagle spread his wings and flew, spiralling up and up until he was only a tiny speck in the clear, hot sky. Eagle flew and flew, for hours and hours. It seemed that he would never get there, and he was getting very tired. Then he saw a light and flew towards it. He had arrived at Great Spirit's lodge.

"Is anyone there?" said Eagle.

A big booming voice said, "Come in."

Eagle opened the flap and walked in.

When Great Spirit saw that Eagle was very sad, he asked, "What news do you bear?"

Eagle moaned. "The people are suffering. They cannot catch game or find plants to eat, and the rivers and lakes are drying up."

Great Spirit tried to think of what he could do to help. While he thought, he grew sadder every minute until he burst into tears, big tears that rained down to earth. The plants returned and the animals came to feast on them. Hunting trips were rewarded with food for all.

Now, whenever it gets dry, Great Spirit cries, and it rains on the earth.

Kevin Dietzel :: Grade 7
Long Prairie/Grey Eagle Public School :: Long Prairie

TREES

I am Tidnab. I am part fox and part bat. I am the god of thieves. I live in a land with no shadow to keep the tribe cool; the villagers will surely die soon.

Once, long ago, people had to hold up their own shadows. Then they disappeared. My friends and I are going to find a shadow which will stand up without someone holding it.

The sun god, who is part lion and part unicorn, was standing on a plateau shining his rays down upon the village. Just then Drib, the beaver-bird, flew to the plateau.

"Why are you shining down on the villagers when you know there is no shadow to protect them," Drib inquired.

"Because without light," the sun god said, "the tribe cannot hunt for the food which they need to survive."

I was flying overhead, evesdropping on the sun god and Drib. After hearing what the sun god was doing, and why, I swooped down to put in my own two cents.

"Ah, Tidnab," said the sun god, gesturing. "And what brings you here?"

"Everything but you," I joked.

"We need a shadow for the village," said Drib.

"And how can we go about this?" the sun god asked.

And with this, I took some dirt and formed it into a thick base that branched out at the top. "You see," I announced, "we need something that can grow out of the ground."

"We also need something that will make the shadow look nice," said Drib. With that, I whisked some grass off the plateau and molded it into the branches of the dirt. The three of us made many more of these and created a large shadow over the village.

So when you sit under a tree to keep cool on a sunny day, please remember how they came into the world.

Aimee J. Wendt :: Grade 7
Long Prairie/Grey Eagle Public School :: Long Prairie

UNTITLED

Where did a football go when someone put clothes on it?
To the fan club.

Who ate flowers in the field?
A field mouse.

Why do dolphins check into a hotel?
To get more sleep.

How do ants celebrate their birthdays?
With crumbs.

Where do dreams go in the morning?
To your stomach.

Why are there people?
There are people because nature intended to have us.

Why is your foot shaped the way it is?
You need a shoe to fit it.

Where does music go when it is not being sung?
In your mouth.

When does a fish sleep?
When it's too fat and full to swim.

Where does darkness go at dawn?
It fades.

Why do ants talk to each other?
They make plans for food.

What do tigers think of when they go to sleep?
Meat.

When does a desk eat?
When it hungers for supplies.

Why does a flag stand still?
Because it has no place to go.

Ms. Brandvold's Class :: Grade 4
Parkway Elementary School :: St. Paul

"But why can't I go? asked Gorb.

"No, you're just too young. I'm sorry," answered Geozy.

Geozy turned around and walked away. Gorb, jumping up and down on his one foot, and flailing his arms in the air, finally sat down and started to think. I'm smarter than them, they're just bigger and stronger than me, thought Gorb. I really want to get off this planet. Ha! If I can't go, then I'm not going to let them go.

As the musty wind blew over the launch pad where Gorb sat, he thought to himself, How am I ever going to stop them from leaving? There's no way I could ever capture them. Gorb looked across the launch pad. He was staring at the Boab X-2 spacecraft. I know all about that spaceship. They're still learning, Gorb thought to himself. Ah, I have an idea. He got up and started toward the ship.

Meanwhile Geozy, the leader of this sector on Planet Zorbulaxi-tive, was talking with Halipanyania and Calvizip, the other two elders.

"We just can't bring Gorb, he's too young. Yes, he knows every-thing about the ship, but that's not good enough," said Geozy. He hopped on his one foot to the other side of the pit, where Calvizip was preparing their dinner: fried zebballies in delmn sauce, slugs in ketchup.

"Smells good, Calvizip," complimented Geozy, while picking one up and swallowing it whole. "And they taste good too!"

"But what if we take him and he helps us out. We don't totally know about Boab X-2. What if something goes wrong, and we don't know what to do? Gorb can help us!" protested Halipanyania.

"Think of it this way. What if something happens, and Gorb doesn't know what to do? I don't want to be responsible for his death," said Geozy. "We're not going to talk about it anymore, and that's final!" He slapped this three-fingered hand on the table in anger.

"That's fine, dinner's ready, let's eat!" said Calvizip anxiously.

Back at the launch pad, Gorb was looking up at the now opened control panel under Boab X-2. He thought to himself, as he scratched the top of his head with his three long green fingers, Hmmm, now how can I manage this? The green wire runs the windshield wipers, the red runs the radio, the black runs the heat . . . Ahh! There it is, the blue wire! If I cut this one, it will cut out any and all power. All I have to do is take these scissors, and . . . His thought was cut short as he sensed Geozy walking up behind him. Geozy, still eating a zebbaly, shouted to Gorb, "What are you doing under there!"

"Nothing," said Gorb nervously. He quickly closed the control panel.

"Yah you were. You were going to destroy the ship, hoping that we couldn't figure out how to fix it, weren't you?" asked Geozy accusingly.

"No, no I wasn't!" protested Gorb.

"Then why are you holding those scissors? What were you planning on doing, giving the ship a haircut, like trimming the wires up?"

Geozy walked over to Gorb, took the scissors and threw them point down into the ground. He took some rope out of his pocket. He tied it around Gorb's hands. Then he led Gorb back to the pit. While they were walking back, Gorb slipped free and headed for the Zorbulaxitive National Forest. But Geozy, being bigger and swifter, quickly gained ground and recaptured Gorb. They headed for the pit again, this time Geozy carrying Gorb over his shoulder. They finally got back to the "Elder Pit" where Calvizip and Halipanyania were waiting for Geozy. They were sitting at the dinner table at the bottom of the pit, finishing up the zebballies.

"Why did you leave so suddenly?" asked Halipanyania.

"I had this sudden urge to check the ship. Look who I found just seconds away from destroying it," said Geozy proudly.

"Whoa!" screamed Cal and Hal, so in unison it was almost funny.

"What should we do with him now?" asked Cal.

As Geozy jumped into the pit, he set Gorb down on the table.

"We're just going to have to keep watch on him until we leave," said Geozy, "I've made up my mind, we're not going to leave until three days from now. Hopefully by that time, we'll understand the entire ship."

"Okay, but who's going to watch him?" asked Hal.

"You will," said Geozy. "You're the smallest one here. That

reminds me. I've decided that you're going to stay here when Cal and I go to Earth."

"I don't like this, but if it's in the group's best interest, I'll stay," said Hal, showing some anger in his voice.

"It is. Cal and I are going to go learn some more about the ship," said Geozy as he and Cal jumped up out of the pit onto higher ground. They headed for the launch pad.

When Gorb was sure that they couldn't hear him, he began to talk to Hal.

"Hey Hal. You know they're screwing you just like me. They take the shortest ones and throw them away like yesterday's garbage," said Gorb.

"They're just doing this for the good of the group," Halipanyania said back.

"That's what they said to me. Look how I am now!"

"What?! You sound like you have an idea for us to be able to go to earth," said Halipanyania.

"Yah, and what's it to you?" asked Gorb.

"Well, I really do want to go to earth. What's your idea?"

"If you take this rope off of my hands, maybe I'll tell you," said Gorb.

Halipanyania reached over and untied the extremely tight knot.

"Okay, what is it?" asked Halipanyania.

"Since I know all the parts of this ship, and I can't destroy it, I'm thinking of a plan B. It involves building a whole new spacecraft, maybe even adding a new feature or two. Since they're planning on leaving in three days, we have to hurry if this is even going to be worth it!"

"I like that plan," said Halipanyania in amazement.

"Let's go. I have all the parts I need in my pit in the forest," said Gorb. "It's the greatest place for hiding my things."

Halipanyania picked up Gorb, jumped up to the edge, set Gorb down, then followed him into the forest.

Meanwhile, Geozy and Calizip are discussing the trip at the ship.

"How come you decided not to bring Halipanyania? He's part of our group," asked Calvizip.

"I felt that he's still too young. He's also behind us, way behind us in learning how to run this thing. Maybe next time," answered Geozy.

"Okay, it just seems kind of mean. Can you trust him to watch Gorb?"

"I don't know. Perhaps this will prove whether or not we can trust him."

In the meantime, Gorb and Halipanyania have reached the pit in the forest. "You're right, there is a lot of stuff here. It looks like you could build fifty ships!" said Halipanyania anxiously.

"No, actually all these parts go together to make just one ship. Let's get to work!" said Gorb.

So over the next two days, they worked and worked. They slept a few hours in between, ate some zebballies, and talked and worked some more. On the second night, they finally finished. They planned to sleep for a few hours before leaving in the morning. What they didn't know was that Geozy and Calvizip had been looking for them. Geozy and Cal gave up the search. It was the second night and they believed they knew everything about the ship. When they were looking for Gorb and Hal, they tested each other about it.

Gorb and Hal were sleeping in their pit, and Geozy and Cal were sleeping in the "Elder Pit."

The sun rose quickly the next morning, the day of the launches. Gorb, looking over his ship, noticed some mechanical problems. He told Hal that they were going to have to delay till noon, while he made the repairs.

Back at "Elder Pit," Geozy and Cal got up. They were planning on eating before their noon launch. Cal, who was turning out to be a great cook, threw some more zebballies onto the frying pan.

Once they had finished their meal, it was a few minutes before noon, just enough time to get to the launch. They casually strolled to the launch pad. They were just about to board when they heard an explosion. They turned toward the forest where the noise came from. All of a sudden a ship came soaring up from the tree tops. As it shot higher and higher, it exploded. Geozy knew instantly that it was Gorb and Halipanyania and that there was no way they could have survived that explosion.

Geozy said to Calvizip, "I hope this teaches you a lesson; 'Never disobey your elders.' "

Marc LaLiberte :: Grade 9
West Junior High School :: Hopkins

Before the play begins, two ARTISTS quickly draw on the backdrop (chalkboard) a picture of a cave in the desert.

NARRATOR: Scene one. The desert.

[Five WOLVES are in a cave growling at each other, and nipping at each other's fur. Slowly they fall asleep, except one. He wanders outside. The MOON rises.]

MOON: I'm coming up again. Goodnight people. (to the WOLF:) Don't howl.

WOLF: (howls) Ow-oooo. . .

MOON: Don't howl.

WOLF: Ow-ooooo. . .

MOON: Shut up.

WOLF: Ow-ooo. . .

[The MOON jolts the WOLF with some power. The WOLF falls on his back, knocked out.]

NARRATOR: Scene two. Under the Earth.

[While the WOLF lies there, the two ARTISTS erase the picture of the cave, and draw flames and smoke. This takes ten seconds. Three DEVILS enter, and find the WOLF lying there.]

DEVIL 1: What's this?

DEVIL 2: How did this get here?

[The WOLF wakes up, growls at the DEVILS. They are afraid of him. He bites at them. They all run away in circles as he chases each of them. They circle around him, and cast a spell, waving him upwards.]

DEVILS 1 and 2: Up to Heaven. Up to Heaven.

DEVIL 3: Get out of here.

[The WOLF slowly stands, as if floating upwards. He floats.]

NARRATOR: Scene three. Heaven.

[The two ARTISTS erase the flames and smoke and draw clouds and stars. Three ANGELS enter.]

ANGEL 1: Look! What is that?

ANGEL 2: How did he get here?

[The WOLF suddenly snaps at them. ANGEL 3 runs away to get GOD.]

ANGEL 3: God, come quick. One of your creatures is biting and growling at us.

[GOD Enters.]

GOD: (to WOLF:) Yo. Sit. Sit.

[The WOLF growls at him, looking ready to jump on him.]

GOD: Yo. What did I say? Sit. Sit up. Yo boy. Sit up.

[The WOLF bites at GOD. GOD runs away.]

GOD: (running away) Get that mutt out of here!

[The ANGELS flap their wings at the WOLF to blow him into outer space.]

ANGELS: Get out of here, you mutt.

[WOLF floats into space. ANGELS exit.]

NARRATOR: Scene four. Outer space.

[The two ARTISTS erase the picture of heaven, and draw a picture of outer space. A sun floats by, burning the WOLF. A black hole enters and sucks the WOLF in, then spits him out. Finally a comet enters, and crashes into the WOLF. Both the WOLF and the comet explode. We see the leg bone of the WOLF floating. We hear a voice:]

BONE: I was a bone inside a wolf. The wolf howled at the moon. All of a sudden I was bounced from place to place. Then it felt like a school hit me. The skin split open. Now I'm having the time of my life floating around.

Matt Stemwedel and Mr. Schreifel's Class :: Grade 6
Pullman Elementary School :: St. Paul Park

Upstage, away from the audience, a table with MOM, DAD and SIS-
TER eating pancakes. Down stage, closer to the audience, is TJ's room
with two beds. He sleeps in one of them. Attached to the wall above
the other bed there are small musical instruments and doll house furni-
ture. Silence as TJ sleeps. Then the instruments begin to play "When
the Saints Go Marching In." TJ awakens, goes over to investigate the
music. As he steps on the bed, a SKELETON rises from it, grabs him
roughly and drags him to the other wall in the room.

TJ: Stop!

SKELETON: I'm dragging you to your destiny!

TJ: Where? Why? What if I don't want to?

SKELETON: You don't have a choice. There is something very
important for you this way.

[SKELETON drags TJ to the wall, and pushes him through it.]

SKELETON: GO!

[TJ is in the darkness.]

TJ: I hope this doesn't take too long. I might miss breakfast.

[A blinding light switches on him. A MAN is there.]

MAN: Step forward.

TJ: Yes. Yes sir.

MAN: Are you the one they call TJ?

TJ: Yes. Yes. I think so, sir.

MAN: What took you so long? I've been waiting forever.

TJ: I—I don't know, sir.

MAN: This is the beginning of your spiritual cleansing.

[He holds a mirror to TJ's face. In the mirror, TJ sees his body
lying in the bed in his room. The lights come up on his bed with a
body lying in it.]

TJ: That's me. But—I'm here.

MAN: Your spirit is here. There is your earthly being. While you are here being cleansed, someone else will take your place there.

TJ: But why must I be cleansed? Did I do something wrong? Does everyone have to do this? I'm so confused.

MAN: Slow down. One at a time. You were sent here because in your life you were picked to do a very great thing. You are supposed to lead a revolution. Thousands of people are counting on you. We must make sure you are of sound mind and body.

TJ: How long will this take? I don't want to be gone too long.

MAN: Nobody will even know you are gone.

TJ: But all the same, will this cleansing be painful? I don't like pain much.

MAN: You mustn't be a wimp. You are to be a great leader. We must go.

[Light change as the MAN leads TJ to a room full of candles.]

TJ: Wow. This is really cool. What's it used for?

MAN: This is where we do our praying and meditating.

TJ: Medi–what–ing?

MAN: Cleansing your mind. Taking thoughts and ideas into your soul.

TJ: Sounds too complicated.

MAN: If you're not willing—

[He moves away. TJ grabs him.]

TJ: I am. I want to lead and be great.

[From the Kitchen, the MOTHER calls. It sounds like a loud noise, not like a voice calling.]

TJ: What was that?

MAN: Nothing. Never mind.

[The noise again. The lights all fade to black. The MAN, the can-

THE DREAM OF THE WHALE :: 117

dles, everything disappears except the table of PEOPLE eating pancakes. Lights come back up on TJ sitting up in his bed.]

TJ: Man, that was a weird dream.

[He finds the mirror. He looks in. We hear the MAN's voice, as if it comes from the mirror. TJ sees the MAN in the mirror.]

MAN: Shall we keep going?

TJ: AHHHH! (blackout)

T. J. Berning and Lieann Campbell :: Grade 7
Willmar Junior High School :: Willmar

Wisdom

There are two kinds of wisdom
The kind you want to hear and the kind you don't
Your grandma gives the one you want to hear
Your grandpa gives the kind you don't
My grandma's words are,
"eat more"
"sleep late"
"just as long as you try hard"
"there's nothing wrong with C's"
My grandpa's words are just the opposite,
"eat less"
"get up earlier"
"try harder"
"Try harder"
"C's stink"
Both are good but you
have to balance them

Ryan Carroll :: Grade 7
Mahtomedi Middle School :: Mahtomedi

Run Sisters Run

Run sisters run
Run with your brothers
Not behind, not ahead
but right beside each other
but right beside each other

Treat us fair
Boys and girls
Everybody wants to be equal in this world
All we're saying, we don't want to complain
but everybody should be treated the same

Women did the work
Men got the glory
in the olden days
That was the same old story
Women couldn't vote, men didn't care
Women didn't get to do what was fair

Girls like pink, boys like blue
I've heard a lot of people say it's not true
Boys can like pink, girls can like blue
whatever color you like is up to you

We declare changing times
At school, at home, in nursery rhymes
Sports and business, colors and clothes
Toys we play with and TV shows

Ms. Pettit's Class :: Grade 5
Caledonia Elementary School :: Caledonia

Fourteen year old Jodeci flung open the door of her home in Bloomington, MN, smiling happily.

"Mom, Dad, I'm home!" she called as she tossed her coat on the floor.

"Pick up your coat and put it away!" her mother called back from an unseen room in the house.

Jodeci threw up her hands in exasperation and picked up her coat and put it away. "Figures," she muttered.

"Hiya, kid," her sixteen year old brother Shane said as she turned the corner and as he tugged on her long blond hair.

She scowled at his back as he walked away. She headed for her room just as the phone rang shrilly.

"I'll get it!" Jodeci shrieked as she raced for the phone. "Hello?" she panted into the phone.

"Just come in from a long run?" came her friend Brooke's voice over the line.

"No . . . I . . . ran . . . to . . . pick . . . up . . . the . . . phone . . . !" she gasped.

"You are too strange, Jodi," Brooke said.

Jodeci could almost see her rolling her big, blue eyes.

"Anyways, I was wondering if you want to come over," Brooke asked.

"Well, hold on. I'll ask. Mom! CAN I GO TO BROOKE'S?" Jodeci hollered.

Her mother appeared at the doorway wiping her hands on a dish-towel. "Honey," she paused, looking troubled. "We have to have a talk tonight," she said quietly.

Jodeci slowly returned the receiver to her ear. "I can't," she said abruptly.

"But why?" Brooke whined. "I have tons of things planned. I wanted to call Mike. You can see my new CD's and . . ."

Jodeci cut her off. "I told you I can't," she snapped.

"Okay, okay," Brooke said sulkily. "Have it your way."

The line went dead after the slam of Brooke's phone.

Jodeci sighed, replacing the phone to its cradle. She wondered what was so important that her mother had to say. Maybe I don't want to know, she thought. A feeling of dread had come over her.

Dinner had arrived and the only sound was the clinking of silverware on plates. Jodeci pushed her food around on her plate. Her mother wiped her mouth with her napkin and turned to Jodeci's father.

"Mark, should we tell them?" she asked hesitantly.

"Well, it's either now or never." He set down his silverware. "Jodi, Shane, we have some news for you."

Well, duh! Jodeci thought, raising one eyebrow at her brother. He looked just as confused.

"We're moving," her mother blurted out.

Jodeci's green eyes widened and she dropped her fork. Her brother looked dazed. Her father cleared his throat.

"You've got to be joking. And if you are, it's a pretty nasty joke," spat Jodeci.

"Hon, I'm afraid it's not," her mom said quietly.

Jodeci jumped up and ran to her room and slammed the door. Soon after she heard the sound of her brother's door slamming, too. Jodeci cried herself to sleep.

ONE WEEK LATER

Jodeci stared into space. She's not spoken to her mother in a week. A soft knock on her door sounded. "Jodi, we need to talk," came her mother's voice. Her mother, father and brother walked in.

"Jodi, we decided to decide as a family whether to move or not. It wasn't fair to spring that on you," said her mother. "We'll do anything to get our Jodi back."

Jodeci raised her eyes to her mom's. "Do you mean it?" she asked.

Her mom smiled. "Of course."

Jodeci jumped up and hugged her, her dad, and—very surprisingly —her brother.

Kelly Doyle :: Grade 8
Hidden Oaks Middle School :: Prior Lake

I am sitting in the corner of a dark room. I look at my arms and I see that they are covered with soft, long, fuzzy fur. This fur is a very drab color.

Oh, no!

Pitter-patter! Pitter-patter! A blond-haired, blue-eyed, short little monster was coming at me!

What is he going to do to me? He picks me up and squeezes me tight. He's bringing me towards a square, a dark glass square. It looks outside into the night. I wonder what those flashes of light are.

Little drops of wetness, tiny little drops, they're coming faster now! What is that awful noise?

I know!

He's crying! What is he crying about? I wish I could speak out loud and ask him, but I can't so I suppose I'll never know.

I guess all I can do is give him—

A HUG!

Melissa Scarela :: Grade 7
Long Prairie/Grey Eagle Public School :: Long Prairie

DAVID'S TANTRUM

Once there was a boy named David and David threw tantrums. Every day when he was outside in the field with the cows, all of a sudden David threw a tantrum. He started to scream and shout and kick his legs. His thirteen year old sister came out and said, "That David sure has a temper." Then David would scream at her. David got up and started to work. Sometimes he would work too hard. If something didn't go his way, he would run out to the field and throw a tantrum. And the cows would start mooing. David's clothes were all dirty because he threw tantrums. David's mother always said, "Now, David, I must wash your overalls today." But David would answer, "No way, Mom. I will never wash them." David went in the house and his mother would say, "Your overalls, please." But again David would answer, "No way, Mom. I will never wash them." David's mother would scream at him and David would throw a fit, run out to the cow's pen, and throw a tantrum. The cows would bellow at David because of the noise he made. After that, it was time to go to school. He didn't change out of his overalls. Instead, he went to school with them on. At school people started teasing David because he was so dirty. He began to cry and then instead of running home he threw a fit in the hall. The principal called David's mom. David's mom came to pick him up and usually he screamed, but this time he didn't. When they got home David said, "Please wash my overalls." So David's mother did. David said, "It's time I grew up." So after that David never threw a tantrum again.

Sarah Anderson :: Grade 4
Cedar Creek Community School :: Cedar

ROCKY JIM

NARRATORS: Once upon a time there was a boy named Rocky Jim.

[ROCKY JIM swaggers to the center of the stage and looks around to see if anyone is watching him.]

NARRATORS: Rocky Jim sometimes did bad things. He threw rocks at cars.

[ROCKY JIM pushes two of the rocks at the car.]

CAR TIRE #1: Ouch.

CAR TIRE #2: Ssssssss.

[Second car tire goes flat.]

NARRATORS: And ignored his parents when they told him to stop.

PARENTS: Rocky Jim, stop throwing rocks at cars.

NARRATORS: One day his next door neighbor spoke to him.

NEXT DOOR NEIGHBOR #1 (approaching): Rocky Jim, why do you throw rocks at cars?

ROCKY JIM (smart-mouthed): Because I want to.

NEXT DOOR NEIGHBOR #2 (approaching): Come on Rocky Jim. Stop it!

ROCKY JIM: No. I don't have to.

[The REAR TIRES stand up and re-inflate their friend.]

ALL CAR TIRES (in unison): Let's throw rocks at Rocky Jim and see how he likes it. Maybe he'll learn that it's not nice to hit anyone or anything.

[They all rock rocks at ROCKY JIM.]

ROCKY JIM: What's happening, oh my gosh. Help, help! This can't be real. I hope I'm dreaming.

ALL CAR TIRES (in unison): This is not a dream and if you'll stop throwing rocks at cars, we'll be tires again.

ROCKY JIM: Okay, I'll stop.

PARENTS: Do you promise?

ROCKY JIM: All right.

NEIGHBORS (in unison): We're glad you stopped.

NARRATORS: And Rocky Jim never threw rocks again.

Ms. Marshall's Class :: Grade 1
North End Elementary School :: St. Paul

I'm Sorry

Scene 1: The TOWN BULLY is feeling sad and angry about how the town feels about him. He walks outside of town and passes by a cave. He walks into the cave. He sees a FLOWER that looks like fire.

BULLY: Hey. What's that? I can take it.

> [He bends down to pick the FLOWER, but it suddenly throws fire all over him.]

Scene 2: Outside the cave. The BULLY'S BONES stumble out of the cave, and fall into a pile. As they fall, they turn to black jewels. The BULLY'S SHADOW walks out of the cave and sees the bone pile.

SHADOW: Hey. That's my bones. How do I get my bones back?

> [A flying FAIRY enters.]

FAIRY: You have to apologize to the town. You have to apologize to the town.

Scene 3: The SHADOW walks to town, which is played by the audience. He apologizes to person after person in the town. Each PERSON stands up and accepts the apology in one way or another. The SHADOW walks back to the cave. He goes inside. He walks into the fire. The BONE PILE gets up from outside the cave, and runs into the fire. The BULLY, now a new person with new bones, walks out of the fire and out of the cave.

BULLY: Hey. I'm different.

Ms. Sterud's Class :: Grade 5
Lakeview Elementary School :: Robbinsdale

VIOLENCE, STOP

I was setting the table
on Saturday night
with gold and silver
beneath the light.
I heard a cry,
it sounded nearby.
I smelled the violence
in the air,
I ran over to stare.
I saw a very scary sight,
my sister and brother
were beginning to fight.
I yelled, "This isn't right."
Usually I am the one
who's outspoken,
but I didn't want
to see my family trust broken.
I made them stop
their kicking and tugging
and made them apologize
and start hugging.

Because violence is
becoming a curse,
keep your family
and don't let
it get worse.

Keara Prom :: Grade 4
Greenleaf Elementary School :: Apple Valley

Think of what they said to me:
    Bounce, bounce . . . Swish.
Think of what they did to me:
    Clank, clank . . . Bounce.
Building up inside of me:
    Bounce, clank . . . Swish.
Couldn't hold it inside, I think
of the angry words while I
    Bounce, bounce, clank . . . Swish.
Cooler now:
    Dribble, dribble . . . Swish!

John Crosser :: Grade 8
Central Middle School :: Columbia Heights

Based on a dream by Vue Dang, developed by the class.

Stage Right: The SUN (played by two people)

Stage Left: The BUDDAH, sitting peacefully on a cloud.

Up Center: The WIFE, sitting cross-legged, smiling.

Down Right: A TREE (played by one person)

A MAN enters. The SUN shines on him, and gives him power. He swells up with power. The SUN gives him more and more. The MAN pulls out a huge cigarette (a foot long), and lights it on the SUN. He is very powerful now, and struts around proudly. Then he turns to a TREE, and he gestures powerfully towards it. The TREE shakes, then cracks loudly and falls over. The MAN is very proud of himself. The WIFE cries.

WIFE: I didn't know my husband was so powerful.

BUDDAH: Ha-Ha-Ha-Ha.

> [WIFE goes to HUSBAND. She stares deeply into his eyes, and his power begins to drain from him and transfer to the WIFE. The MAN begins to die.]

MAN: You traitor! Why do you . . . Kill me? I . . . am your . . . husband!

WIFE: You killed someone so you must be killed.

MAN: It was just a tree.

WIFE: It was my favorite tree.

> [MAN dies. WIFE has his power. She struts around proudly. BUDDAH gets up from his cloud, and goes to the WIFE.]

BUDDAH: Ah-me-DHA-phut. (Translation: Blessings on you.) You killed your husband, so I will take away your power.

WIFE: You can't. You can't.

> [They lock eyes, stare at each other. BUDDAH, since he is so old,

dies. The sun sees this, and starts taking back the power from the WIFE. The WIFE cries out in pain each time the SUN takes a piece of power back.]

SUN: You killed your husband.

WIFE (pain): Ah! EE! AI!

SUN: I now take back all the power.

WIFE (dying): Ah! I'm so sorry! EEE! I'm so sorry! EE! AI! EE!AI!

[dies]

O!

Ms. Mau's ESL Class :: Grades 7–9
Kellogg Junior High School :: Rochester

THE TRUTH

He is the Truth
raging battles
across the universe.
The truth is as old as the universe
weaving a pattern through time.

The truth's paws smash
the veil of time
flying through on his powerful wings.

The truth's call is like a thousand lions
roaring in the night.

I see the truth
pounding across the sand.
I see him
winging across the endless sky,
all to battle.

He is the Griffin.

The Griffin with his eyes
of midnight coal.
The Griffin with his wings of steel.
The Griffin's paws as soft as pillows
though they're swift as the wind.
The Griffin with his body of rock
able to withstand sword and arrow.

He is the warrior of truth.

Joel Martin :: Grade 5
Meadowbrook Elementary School :: Hopkins

NARRATOR: A long long very very long time ago, there was a tribe of people. These people could become animals if they wanted to, and they could become people again whenever they wanted to. Everyone lived together happily. On certain days of the month or year they would all go to the center of the village, and they would watch each other dance.

NARRATOR: But then, something bad started to happen to the tribe. Tornadoes swept through the village and wiped out houses. Lightning struck the village and many people were electrocuted. Fires started and some people were burned. The tribe called out, "Who will save us?"

TRIBE: WHO WILL SAVE US?

NARRATOR: The chief gathered everyone together and made them vote for either the panther, the eagle or the cheetah.

[PEOPLE hold up their hands as if to vote.]

NARRATOR: The cheetah was elected to leave the village and go on a journey to try to find a solution to this turmoil. But there was disagreement from the tribe. Some refused to vote. A wolf person stoodup.

WOLF PERSON: I won't vote for any of them because it is the wolf who should save the village.

OTHER WOLF PEOPLE: Yes! The wolf. The wolf should be the one!

CHIEF: We will see who can run the fastest, the wolf or the cheetah. The winner will go to save the village.

TRIBE PERSON: We don't have time for tests. See, even now, the tornadoes are coming again. The lightning is coming. We need to decide, now!

CHIEF: Then the wolf and the cheetah will go together to save the village.

TRIBE PEOPLE: Yes. Yes. Good idea.

WOLF PERSON: No! Only the wolf. The wolf should go alone.

NARRATOR: There was great trouble in this village. The chief made a decision. The wolf would go on a journey to find a solution to the tribe's problem. The wolf was strong and ferocious, and could attack and fight. But the wolf would be accompanied by the cat. The cat was small and graceful. It could fit into small places, and jump and climb in narrow places. The chief knew they would make a good team. But the wolf and the cat did not get along very well.

[The WOLF and CAT enter.]

WOLF: Get out of my way, you stupid cat. (Plus more insults.)

CAT: Stop calling me names. (Plus more insults.)

NARRATOR: The wolf and the cat came to a bridge leading to a cave with many doors. At the mouth to the cave stood a strange goat.

[The WOLF and CAT come to a bridge. On the bridge is a GOAT. A laughing GOAT. Beyond the GOAT and the bridge is a cave with many doors. The WOLF and CAT are arguing so much that they don't even notice the GOAT. They circle around the GOAT insulting each other. The GOAT finally touches each of them and they are paralyzed and fall asleep. The GOAT rises up, and flies around them laughing. The GOAT laughs hard at them, as if to say "So there—now you noticed me." The GOAT leaves through one of the doors. Sound of door opening and closing. The WOLF and CAT wake up. They try to open a door, but cannot.]

CAT: How the heck did we get in here?

WOLF: Why did you come and get us in this mess?

[Door opens. GOAT enters.]

WOLF: Who are you?

CAT: What do you want from us?

GOAT: I want gold. And I want your head.

[The WOLF and the CAT talk quietly to each other.]

WOLF: I'm not giving up my head.

CAT: I'm not giving up my head.

GOAT: I want gold. And I want your head.

CAT: Look, how about a tail? I'll give you my tail.

WOLF: No. Don't do that.

CAT: Remember why we are here. We have to find a way to help the others. (To the goat:) I'll give you my tail.

[The WOLF is amazed by the CAT's action.]

WOLF: Are you sure about that?

CAT: Yes.

WOLF: Why are you doing this?

CAT: For our tribe.

WOLF: I could never give up my tail.

[WOLF bites off the CAT's tail. This is done slowly, to show how reticent the WOLF is to bite it off, and how painful it is for the CAT. The GROUP makes a bite noise and a squeal noise.]

GOAT: You go through that door to find what you need to help your people. I will hide your tail here. When you come back, if you can guess which door the tail is behind, you can take it with you.

[WOLF and CAT go through a door. The GOAT dances happily holding the tail (or CAT's other hair) on his bald head.]

GOAT: I finally have some hair. I finally have some hair. HA HA HA.

[He exits.]

NARRATOR: Through the door, the wolf and the cat find a tiny door. They pick it up and look at it closely. The wolf and cat took the door back to the tribe. It took a long time, and they had many adventures. But we can't tell about them all right now.

[WOLF and CAT enter the circle.]

WOLF: We return!

CAT: We have quite a tale to tell.

WOLF: You don't have a tail.

CHIEF: Quickly! Give us what you have found. Look how everyone is arguing!

TRIBE PERSON 1: See the tornados!

TRIBE PERSON 2: And the lightning.

[The GROUP argues, and a tornado and lightning bolt strike.]

CAT: Here is the door.

EVERYONE: A door?

WOLF: When the tornado and the arguments come, we cut off a piece of the door, and throw it into the sky, and the weather will calm down.

PERSON 4: That's stupid.

PERSON 5: You failed.

PERSON 6: They did not.

PERSON 7: Shut up.

EVERYONE: Shut up. You shut up. You shut up . . . etc. . . .

[The tornado comes again. People keep arguing. The WOLF and CAT cut a piece off the door and throw it into the sky. The arguing stops and the weather calms.]

Ms. Nelson's Class :: Grade 3
Greenvale Park Elementary School :: Northfield

Five Cents More

Once there was this girl who lived in the sewer and her name was Kimberly. She wanted a puppy but her mom said no because they did not have enough money to get a dog and feed it. It would starve.

Kimberly looked in the bright water of the sewer and started to cry because she could not have a dog. But she thought about the other kinds of pets she could have. She thought about a cat, but that had the same problem, and then she had a perfect idea. She thought that a fish would be easy to take care of because fish are only about $1.00 and food was about $2.00, and that equals $3.00. She had just enough money so she went to the pet shop and got herself a fish and she picked out a special fish.

When she went up to the counter to buy the fish, she did not know that there would be tax, and she did not have enough money. She needed five more cents.

But the store clerk knew she wanted a fish really badly, so the clerk took out five cents and gave it to her. Now that she could get the fish she was so happy that her face glowed up. And the store clerk knew that she was a bum and did not have money. The clerk gave her $10.00 to give to her mom and she was so happy her face glowed up even more. Then she ran home and gave it to her mom, and with one dollar of that money they ran out and got a thank you card and they went to the pet shop and gave it to the clerk.

After that, they were friends for a long time, and they got healthy because that special clerk gave them that money.

Stacy Mikel :: Grade 5
Highwood Hills Elementary School :: St. Paul

Give Your Love Away

Be like an iguana,
hide your worries away.
Be like an opossum
hang your trouble upside down.
Be like a river,
take freedom for a far distance.
Stick your trouble to the ground
like mud.
Take your trouble far away
like a rocket.
Give your love away
like a shooting star.
Be like a turtle,
stay away from danger.
Be like a snake, slither from fear.
Take bad feelings away
like a volcano.
Give freedom away,
like a gumball machine.
Be like a hawk, fly for love.
Like a seal, swim to safety.

Levi Taylor :: Grade 3
Fernbrook Elementary School :: Maple Grove

THE SWEET CLARITY OF SOMETHING
WONDERFUL

Scribbles

I'm in my room,
with paper and markers.
I grab the black,
begin to draw.
My wrist gets stiff.
I stop and start
to scribble, pressing
the furious black marker
against the paper
as hard as I can,
taking away my strength.
I stop, ripping and
shredding the paper,
throw it away.
I grab a new sheet
and watch my hand
draw flowers—
I feel again I can
face the world.

Laura Utphall :: Grade 6
Central Middle School :: Columbia Heights

THE CHILD AND THE SNOWMAN

A child can make a snowman
    can make it big and round
    can make a small snowman

Sometimes a snowman can melt
    Sometimes the snow can turn to ice

A child can make snow into a book
    can make a snowman a king
    can make a snowman a person

Sometimes the snow can turn to ice
    A child can turn into a snowman

Sometimes a snowman can melt
    A child can feel like a new child

Phong Do :: Grade 1
Parkway Elementary School :: St. Paul

MUSIC

I hear the sweet clarity of something wonderful,
a pure note comes forth

Suddenly more notes join in a harmonious tune

Music rushes through my head like a swift stream,
the tip-tapping of my feet to an orchestra or rock concert

All music is the same to me—
the birds singing, crickets chirping, cymbals clashing
and crashing
the elegant smooth grace of an old grand piano
with ivory keys
the sound of a school band
music is music is music
the voices of a church choir with bells
heavy metal scratching my brains out

Most enjoyed by me is the music I make—
the peaceful recorder, boisterous trumpet or
the rolling piano

> Music is an essentiality to me
> Music is my uplift in life
> Music is my uplift in life

Matt Moody :: Grade 8
Oltman Junior High School :: St. Paul Park

UNCOUNTED

"I love you . . ."
not a time goes by,
". . . a bushel and a peck . . ."
that I don't think about
". . . a bushel and a peck . . ."
my grandpa
". . . and a hug around the neck . . ."

he brought to me,
for every
uncounted
smile,
a story,
a life in every song.
his scratchy voice
repeating
words,
chanting verse.

a doctor,
a well,
another story,
since forgotten,
many tales
yet to be told.

my songs,
sung back
true,
far from him,
too muffled by the
earth

he hears me
still
enchanted.
his hidden many talents
hidden in me also . . .

a story
to be finished,
a song
of life
begun.

Dana Hanson :: Grade 9
Stillwater Junior High School :: Stillwater

I feel white as I see the light catch in a sad tear.
I feel white as I see light scatter through the trees wrangled
branches, and see the dove weave through them so graceful, so light
I feel white when I feel snowflakes drift slowly on my warm face,
to cool it, reassure it that the world is at peace.
I feel white as I stare at a baby's unmarred face, perfection, so
envious of its beauty.
I feel white in the foam from the waves that crash on the ocean's
shore for eternity to tell me all is well.

Elizabeth Saloka :: Grade 5
Katherine Curren Elementary School :: Hopkins

BIRTHDAYS

Birthdays let me
relax in the hot sun.
Birthdays let my friends
and me spit out watermelon seeds
off the deck
and run around in
our swimming suits.
Birthdays are too many
kisses from grandmas.
Birthdays mean more
presents for me me me.
Everyone has to be nice,
even my sister.
Birthdays let me wake up
happy.
They are the color
of the nice sky.
Birthdays mean more
and more love.

Agnes Kim :: Grade 5
Middleton Elementary School :: Woodbury

THINGS I LOVE

I never knew I loved riding the bus,
hearing all the kids screaming
and the bus driver telling them to be quiet,
and whistling with his fingers.
I never knew I loved being myself,
thinking and thinking about everything
that has been going on in my life.
I love the sound of rain beating on my head,
telling me to go in and eat. But why should
I listen to the rain telling me
to go in and eat? I never knew it before.
I love the ceiling, how it looks like it's going to
suck me up and make me light and float away.
That's how it looks. I wish it
was real. I never knew that before.

Amil Henderson-Carr-Thacher :: Grade 4
Christa McAuliffe Elementary School :: Hastings

WHY I LIKE MY COLOR YELLOW

I like my color because it is cool
because I like the sun
sunflowers
lemonade.

I like my color because I like animals
jelly beans
because I like fire
because I like food.

I like my color because I like tents
because I like Jolly Ranchers
because the light
escapes in the morning.

I like my color because I like flowers
bananas
yellow paper
dogs
I like my color
because I like yellow
glowing in the dark
sleeping.

Holly Mazon :: Grade 3
Mill City Montessori School :: Minneapolis

BLACK

What a beautiful color
dark. Like the beauty of
        the night sky
    black.

Not the color of my skin
    but
brown the color of my skin
brown like the sand
across the beach
brown as beautiful as me
    brown.
My eyes and my hair
brown. So beautiful.

Rahshema Sims :: Grade 6
Nettleton Magnet School :: Duluth

My Body Parts

My mind is a deer running down
the brook. My heart is the
love of all the land. My hands are
petals of a flower. My muscles are
the muscles of all the deer.
My bones are the logs for
a home in the woods.
My voice can tell all the people
that danger is coming.
My body can help all the people
that got hurt.

Phillip Miller :: Grade 3
South Elementary School :: St. Peter

STEPHANIE IS AT ONE

She is at one,
one of leadership—
one who takes a stand
that comes out wrong.
She is at one,
rejected by others, liked by some.
Blue-green eyes
as if she were swimming
hundreds of leagues below the sea.
Soft blond hair
that blows in the night.
She is at one,
a sunflower, open and bright.
When she is discouraged,
she is a boulder thrown into the ocean.
But the ocean revises and refreshes her.
She becomes an angel, light,
flowing like a blanket in the wind.
Her mind is a jawbreaker
always revealing new emotions, colors.
She is at one,
at one with herself.

Stephanie Dickey :: Grade 7
Oltman Junior High School :: St. Paul Park

THE DANCE

I dance, my hair is flying around my head.
I don't even notice that I look so stupid.
People around me are dancing. Outside
there's a parade. It sounds so fun, we still
dance, we still hear music, still sing. Now
the music stops. We still sing and dance.
We sing forever, our parents are getting
annoyed. The music starts again, we sing
louder, we dance harder. Now we hear
a song we don't know. We sing something
else, it doesn't sound right, but we don't
care, we're having fun. The people leave,
we sing and dance forever. We'll never stop,
never, we're having fun, we'll never finish.

Jillian Hegstrom :: Grade 6
Crestview Elementary School :: Cottage Grove

Author Index

School Index

Program Writers 1993–1994

Davida Adedjouma
Sigrid Bergie
John Caddy
Florence Chard Dacey
Carol Dines
Margot Fortunato Galt
Dana Jensen
Gita Kar
Roseann Lloyd
Charlie Maguire
Jaime Meyer
John Minczeski
Beverly Acuff Momoi
Sheila O'Connor
Joe Paddock
Stephen Peters
Richard Solly
Deborah Stein
Susan Marie Swanson
Diego Vazquez Jr